Out of the Current

Reclaiming Your Mind, Your Meaning,
and Your Direction

By: Forest of Truth

Table of Contents

Introduction: What Is the Current? 7

    What This Book Is About............................7

    What This Book Is Not 8

    Who This Book Is For 8

    Discomfort Is a Sign of Growth....................9

    Using This Book & Companion Journal.........10

    Before You Begin....................................10

    Author's Note 11

Chapter 1: Born Into the Flow 13

    Shaped Before We Know Ourselves............13

    When Personality Protects.......................15

    You Are Not Broken 16

    Noticing the Water 17

    Water Ebbs and Flows 18

    Chapter Summary 21

Chapter 2: The Invisible Current 22

    Common Destructive Thought Patterns 24

    Scarcity & Comparison 26

    Productivity & Worth 33

    Beliefs About Change.............................34

    Relationships & Love..............................35

    Fear-Based Limitations 37

    Self Criticism & Dismissal 39

Chapter Summary 41

Chapter 3: Shifting Your Focus 42

Transforming Through Pain 42

Shifting Focus and Expanding Potential............. 44

Building a Practice.. 46

Future-Self Vision Prompt 50

Chapter Summary 51

Chapter 4: Moments Become Momentum 53

Maintaining Progress 53

Do What You Can 54

Building Motivation Daily 56

Sustaining Momentum 58

Relaxing Into Progress 59

Momentum Mindset Shifts............................... 60

Chapter Summary... 62

Chapter 5: Wading Through Rapids 63

Experiencing Emotion Like Water...................... 63

Experiencing Emotion Like Fire 65

Embracing Challenging Emotions 66

Emotions As Signals 67

Chapter Summary... 72

Chapter 6: Designing Your Compass 73

The Importance of a Compass........................... 73

Compass vs. Current....................................... 76

Building Directional Habits 77

When the Compass Shifts 78

Your Compass Interacting Externally 79

When the Compass is Cloudy 80

Principles to Consider 82

Chapter Summary 85

Chapter 7: Creating Your Life 86

From Self-Criticism to Curiosity 87

Noticing and Following Resonance 90

Chapter Summary 92

Chapter 8: Tending Relationships 94

Relationships are a Mirror 94

Relationships Require Care 98

Healthy vs Harmful Bonds 102

Selecting Your Relationships 105

Chapter Summary 109

Chapter 9: Connecting to Nature 112

Why Nature Matters 113

Ways to Reconnect 114

Visualizations For Connecting With Nature 116

Chapter Summary 118

Chapter 10: The Purpose Beyond Self 119

From Stabilization to Service 119

Why It Matters to Give 120

Contribution ≠ Sacrifice 121

Listening for What's Yours 122

Sustainable Contribution Through Business 124

Chapter Summary 126

Chapter 11: Turning the Tides 128

Changing Together.. 128

Change is Inevitable 130

Changing Ourselves 131

Change is Necessary 132

Change is Limited.. 133

Navigating with Compassion... 134

Living as Part of the Ecosystem 135

Chapter Summary 137

Chapter 12: The Stream You Choose 139

The Journey Behind You 139

Wiser Waters 139

Returning to Life 140

Building Your Life.. 141

Staying Connected to the Compass................................. 143

Accessing the Flow.. 144

Chapter Summary 145

A Final Offering... 147

Introduction: What Is the Current?

Welcome, and thank you for being here. Whether this book found you during a moment of reflection, a moment of struggle, or your ongoing goal of seeking self-improvement, I want to congratulate you on taking action towards growth. You didn't have to open this. You could have stayed in the current you've known. But here you are, ready to look inward, ask honest questions, and work to attain a deeper sense of choice.

What This Book Is About

Out of the Current is a book about self-honesty, clarity, and intentional change. It's not about optimization, perfection, or high-performance living. It's about defining and following your purpose, while in a place of more balance and peace. And the quiet, courageous work of shifting your way of being so that your life feels more like what you truly want and need, rather than simply what you're used to.

We all live with patterns we defer to when we're running on autopilot, some we are conscious of, while others are not yet on our radar. We are shaped by our childhood circumstances, our family's tendencies and what they modeled to us, the culture we grew up in, and the expectations we were taught to fulfill. These influences don't just touch what we do. They profoundly shape what we notice, what we believe is possible, what we think we deserve, and what we tend to do in moments of stress or uncertainty.

These patterns, when unexamined, become what I'm referring to as **the current**: a powerful, often invisible force that pulls us along, pushes us, carries us, and at times causes resistance in our lives. Sometimes it helps us to go places that are useful. But other times, we find ourselves fighting it because we don't like where it's headed, or drifting in directions we never consciously chose.

This book is about becoming aware of that current and through this clarity, reclaim more power. It's not to become stronger than the current at all times, but to apply wisdom to know when to push against it, when to change, and how to interpret and respond to the currents within yourself and in your life. It's about strengthening your ability to pause, to feel, to understand, and to reorient. It's also about discovering the compass within you that provides your inner sense of direction, your voice, and your values. This inherently results in expanding your capacity to live by them wholeheartedly.

What This Book Is Not

This is not a book about how to win, hustle, or out-achieve. It's not about becoming someone entirely new that is more "successful" than you are now. It's about opening up the dialogue between different aspects of yourself. This means peeling away what isn't you so what remains feels more honest and aligned. It's about creating a new way forward, not through force, but through clarity about what you want, where you want to be, and who you really are. Then, giving that version of you the space to have more impact on your life and the world around you.

Who This Book Is For

If you've ever felt stuck in a pattern that no longer serves you, this book is for you. If you've ever looked at your life and thought, "This doesn't feel quite right," this book is for you. If you know you're capable of change but you're not sure where or how to begin, or you're tired of beginning over and over again, this book is for you.

You don't have to be optimized. You just have to be curious and willing. That's more than enough.

Discomfort Is a Sign of Growth

Throughout this journey, you might find yourself feeling uncomfortable. That's not a problem, that's a sign you're stretching. You're using new muscles. Think of it like exercise. You may not see changes right away, but deep down something is shifting and if you keep at it time will show the results of your effort.

When we begin to see patterns clearly, it can stir grief, shame, fear, or regret. That's normal and you can face it. Let it come. Let it go. These are the growing pains of emotional and spiritual strength. You are building resilience and you are cultivating wisdom.

Different people have different variations and degrees of current to work with and against. It's important to be mindful of this while witnessing our own currents, for two reasons. First, we should practice gratitude and humility by recognizing that others may be fighting much stronger currents than we are and appreciating the advantages or support we do have.

Second, acknowledging our own challenges can deepen our practice of self-compassion and respectful awareness of our journey. These things also matter in planning. It matters with respect to where we go because we must start where we currently are. It helps to realistically estimate how long it could take us to get there, rather than anticipating immediate effects. This is very important to understand, in order to facilitate greater patience and pride about our progress. And for those of us swimming through stronger currents, we often become stronger ourselves as we learn to maneuver the rapids with skill, resilience, and grace.

Using This Book & Companion Journal

Throughout the book, you'll find **reflection prompts**. These are invitations to pause, explore, and integrate the ideas. You can write your responses in this book, in a notebook, or the free PDF:

Before You Begin

You may not always agree with everything in this book. You're not meant to. Take what resonates and leave the rest. Come back to it later if you need to. You are in charge of your journey.

Thank you again for being here, for giving this book a chance, and creating space with your time and presence. I hope these pages help you both soften and build strength. I also hope it helps you to realign your compass, work with your currents rather than fighting them, and find the path meant for you.

<u>Reflection:</u>

- What kind of current have you been swimming in?

- Have you recognized your strength in staying afloat?

- What advantages have you had along the way?

- What strengths have you gained from adversity?

Note: You don't need to answer everything at once, just begin to notice. Awareness is the first stride toward transformation.

Author's Note

I'll be honest with you, despite working on my own self-improvement for over 20 years, writing this was much easier than releasing it.

Like you, I'm still practicing. Still catching myself in old patterns. Still choosing, one day at a time, to move forward with clarity and purpose instead of perfection.

There was a part of me that wanted to wait until everything was polished, certain, and airtight before letting this book go. But that would have meant waiting, not putting this out there where you can read it, and delaying other projects.

So I'm choosing to release this now, not because it's flawless, but because I believe it might meet you where you are, and hopefully help you move forward too.

If you choose to dive further in the book, I hope these pages remind you: you're on your way and you're not alone.

Part I:

Waking Up in the Current

Chapter 1: Born Into the Flow

Before we can change ourselves for the better, we need to understand our current landscape. In this analogy, this means becoming aware of the river we're in, the symbolic flow of our way of being at this time. These currents move us automatically, often beneath the surface of our awareness. When we begin to recognize the flow we're in, we can orient ourselves to the present situation and create space for change.

This chapter explores how we're shaped by early experiences, including circumstantial, familial, cultural, and environmental influences, and how these shape our unconscious beliefs which become the currents we later feel and may at times struggle against. The goal here is not to cast blame but to awaken ourselves to where we are and start to ask questions: Why am I here? Is this where I want to be? Is this way of being preventing me from pursuing meaningful goals, or even from admitting I want them? What do I want, if I really allow myself to go there? What happens when I believe I can eventually change that which might be pushing firmly against me right now?

When we begin to see how we've adapted to the world around us, we gain the power to choose and practice new patterns. You are not broken, where you are is the result of intelligent survival. Now, with compassion and curiosity, we begin the process of observing the flow you've been swimming in and reflecting on where you want to go from here.

Shaped Before We Know Ourselves

Before you had language, you had patterns available to start modeling. You watched, you absorbed, and you adapted. You didn't choose your first ideas about love, safety, anger, or achievement. These were handed to you in how your parents responded to your cries, how teachers corrected you, what the media told you mattered, and so on. You built your internal compass before you knew what one was, and long before you knew you had a choice in the matter.

For some, resistance might come up here and I get it. We get used to ourselves the way we are now. If you become someone new, where would *you* go? What if you miss who you were? Who would you talk to internally, and would you sound different... unfamiliar? If you admit there's room for changing yourself, does it invalidate your existence so far? Well, let's go through these. First of all, you wouldn't be going anywhere. You aren't the habits, you're the observer. You aren't the past, you are the creator of your present. The one who gets to choose what happens in this exact moment. You won't have to miss yourself, because you aren't losing something, you're just adapting again, like you have so many times before. But this time, you're adapting based on your own conscious decisions.

You're always the one in control of your internal world. You will still be interacting as yourself in your own mind. Hopefully, the voice will only grow kinder. You'll have plenty of time to practice habits, to decide if you like them or not before they'll stick. This tends to be true for most people, and at first it can feel frustrating. It usually takes persistence to see habits begin to shift after commitment and practice. It can help to affirm: you are always lovable despite your imperfections yesterday, today, and tomorrow.

The great thing is we get to have free will. This means that despite inevitably sponging up a bunch of habits, tendencies, and beliefs from our surroundings, we can always choose something different and recreate ourselves in the way we would prefer. It takes a lot of work, but isn't that worth it? When you pause to consider the possible rewards for choosing to engage with life differently, the effort begins to feel purposeful... and possible.

Most games we play are for entertainment. Finding fun to distract ourselves from the things we don't like or we're tired of. What if we could find fun in the process of advancing ourselves? This game could change everything foundationally. Can you think of any good reason to not embark on this path, now that you've been called to it? You can go on in your old habits, or become the creator of your life.

When Personality Protects

Sometimes we refer to our own personalities as "just the way I am," when in reality, those behaviors may be self-protective strategies that we have the power to change. For example, second-guessing ourselves before we speak might be a learned way to avoid shame. What might look like laziness in ourselves or others, might actually be the burnout; an exhausted system trying to stay safe by shutting down. Perfectionism, too, is often a signal of a younger self still trying to earn love through being "good enough". What we often label as personality traits may actually be survival strategies. They made sense at the time, and while some may still help us cope, many can quietly keep us from creating the life we truly want.

A lot of the time, people feel trapped in their personalities. This can show up in different ways, sometimes it sounds like "I've always been this way," used as a reason why change isn't possible, especially when it feels hard. Other times, it's a fear of wasting effort after past attempts didn't lead to the results we hoped for. Or maybe there's a deeper fear that trying to change could lead to failure, or even worse, lead into the unsettling unknown. We may also feel a sense of loyalty to our old patterns, as if changing them would mean betraying who we are. But habits, techniques, and tendencies are not our identity. They're just tools we've used. If you only ever use a hammer, everything starts to look like a nail. When you learn to adapt to use the right tool for the job, you become a better carpenter. You are still yourself even as you grow and shift. You don't lose yourself in this freedom, you find yourself.

You Are Not Broken

You didn't fail if your life isn't exactly where you want it today. You simply adapted to your initial circumstances in a way that has outgrown itself. You did what you had to do in an environment that didn't meet all your needs. And now it's not about blaming that environment, it's about seeing it clearly, so you can finally step out of it. When you understand that your coping made sense *then*, you gain the power to choose something new in the *present*.

Not all adaptations are a problem. Some of them serve us well. We rely on them constantly as we go through life. This isn't only true for people; it's true across the natural world. Think about dogs: they adapt to their humans all the time. Over generations, they've even evolved different facial muscles to better communicate with us and we love them for it. In the same way, many of our own adaptations help us survive, connect, and thrive. We don't need to overhaul everything. We simply want to have access to the control panel to grant ourselves awareness and choice. If something's working, if it's neutral or supportive, it doesn't need to be fixed. Focus on changing the adaptations that aren't serving you.

Reflection:

- What coping mechanisms have turned into currents that you aren't happy with anymore?

- What do you think the goal was; how were these habits or behaviors protecting you?

- What situations did they serve you in?

- What would you prefer now - what would you like to replace this belief or behavior with?

- How would that look in a few real-life examples?

Noticing the Water

Imagine being in a river you've inhabited so long, you forgot it's not the only environment that exists. That's what early conditioning does. It feels like reality, not habit and perspective. You might notice moments of this, like waking up during a conversation and realizing you've been nodding along to someone else's opinion without even checking in with your own. But now, we begin the work of seeing even deeper. If you're looking to make massive shifts in your life, that can mean massive effort.

It happens by creating a practice that will stay with you and that you'll use every day to turn the tides. When it feels like too much work, remember, that's a belief too. Alternatively, you could believe it's exactly as much work as it needs to be to enable worthwhile changes. If the outcomes are important to you, why stop? What could be more meaningful to do with your time and energy than building a life aligned with who you truly are? This might be the most courageous and meaningful work you ever do, not just for yourself but also for the world around you. What would happen if more people chose to meet life from that place of serenity, strength, and intention?

Even beyond that, you could believe it's not "hard" at all. You could believe it will take a lot of effort, but applying that effort is not a struggle because it's something you've already decided to do. You don't have to expend energy choosing it again and again. If you start to feel conflict, where things are pulling you away from concentrating your energy toward a goal you've already committed to, you'll address it as it comes. It's work, it's persistence, but you don't have to struggle with the decision. It's simply a matter of meeting the challenges of change with your full attention and belief that you can face them head-on.

Water Ebbs and Flows

Keep in mind, you can always reprioritize.

You don't have to cling to your first instinct or feel locked into any single choice. This journey is about adaptability and learning as you go. If something isn't working, pause and consider whether there's a different route that could be more supportive. Sometimes the best way forward is a small adjustment that realigns you with your bigger vision. You don't have to stick with the first thing you try. You don't want to be rigid, if it means fighting against the same currents indefinitely. Sometimes swimming upstream means you're chasing an old direction or a direction someone else led you down. You can always stop and ask: is this still where I want to go?

Or maybe for you, swimming upstream means you know you want to change your environment. Maybe you saw something that you wanted up river, but now you're past it and just wearing yourself out trying to go backwards. What if instead, you pause to understand what it was that drew you upstream in the first place, why you wanted it, and identify a new and more manageable way to work toward it? Could you approach something similar in a way that feels more aligned, rather than constantly resisting your current reality? You're learning how to better maneuver, to gain leverage in your current environment. That skill will help you move into an environment that supports you more fully. That can take time, but luckily we all have time. We just don't always use it to move toward the places we truly want to go.

With that said, we do all have a limited amount of time. How do you want to be spending yours?

Consider focusing on a limited volume of changes concurrently, so you have adequate energy to follow through. Change requires varying energy depending on the number and complexity of the goals, and it's wise to direct that energy first toward the shifts that are highest on your priority list. If you're choosing several smaller challenges, you might be able to tackle a few simultaneously. But if the shift is major, something that asks a lot of you, consider channeling everything you can into that single effort. As you make progress, things become easier and more natural. You'll gain momentum and, with time, you'll have more bandwidth to take on additional goals or move onto the next one.

<u>Reflection</u>:

- What would building a small practice of change look like for you right now?

- What's one shift you could make, not to fix yourself, but to support who you want to become?

- What fears or beliefs might be telling you that you can't, or shouldn't, change?

- Where do you think those beliefs came from?

- If you let yourself imagine something new, what does it look like?

- What would it feel like to step toward that without judgment?

- How do you want to be using your time on this planet?

Chapter Summary

Many of us carry beliefs that stop us from even trying in areas that matter to us the most. This book is here to help you notice whether that's true in parts of your life, and if it is, to offer guidance for adopting new beliefs that can lead you there. This is about empowering you to embark on the journey that would be most fulfilling for *you*, and to choose each step with intention.

Many people are afraid of making the wrong choice, so they stay stuck in what they know. But what if there isn't a wrong choice? What if most decisions are simply different paths with different costs and benefits? What if it's something you decided to try simply because it was meaningful to you, and that's enough? If you knew on the other side of a decision you would treat yourself with compassion and appreciate whatever came from the experience, would you feel freer to act? You can always learn, course correct, and choose again. And that too, is progress. Now that we've begun to notice the water, we can start choosing how we want to swim.

Chapter 2: The Invisible Current

Most of what shapes our daily lives is invisible. We're not just talking about memories or vague emotions; we're talking about patterns so deeply embedded in our thinking that we barely notice them. They show up as automatic responses, as the paths of least resistance in our choices. Imagine how exhausting and inefficient it would be to have to make all decisions from scratch every time. These subconscious pathways and cognitive shortcuts serve us well sometimes, but what about when the automatic responses aren't leading to where you want to go? These are the invisible currents: the beliefs we've inherited, the cultural norms we've absorbed, and the survival adaptations we've formed over time. They don't always make logical sense, but they carry incredible power.

This chapter is about making those currents more visible to you. Not to judge them but instead to see them, understand where they came from, and ask if they're really serving you anymore. Through this observation you can start moving in a way that new currents form which better suit you.

Before we dive into specific examples, let's lay out a few important guidelines.

First, **this is not about tackling everything at once**. Many people carry a handful of unhelpful beliefs, while others carry dozens. This chapter is not here to overwhelm you, it's here to illuminate. As you explore the examples below, remember that your first job is to prioritize any changes you would like to make. Which ones feel most relevant to you right now? Which ones do you feel ready to face?

First, I would recommend starting with just one to three belief patterns that feel urgent, resonant, or emotionally charged. These might be the ones that most directly impact your daily stress level, self-image, or ability to move forward in the areas you most strongly desire change. You can revisit the others later as you work through the rest of this book.

Second, remember that the goal isn't just to spot these beliefs; it's to shift them. Once a belief is seen, the real work begins. This means replacing it with something more truthful, more empowering, and more aligned with the life you want. By truthful, I don't mean based on your history. I mean that which aligns to the light deep inside you that knows exactly who you really are, beyond everything you've built to get by. We don't want to spend too long studying the weeds. We want to find the roots, clear space, and **plant new thoughts**. When you begin to add foot traffic to the paths you want to take more often in your mind, it makes those routes more accessible and natural to use over time.

Let's begin illuminating the unseen, so you can choose what's next with purpose and power. These are some of the most common hidden beliefs that many people carry, whether consciously or unconsciously. You might recognize just a few, or quite a few, and that's okay. In the pages that follow, you'll find a series of common destructive thought patterns, grouped by theme. You're encouraged to scan through the titles first and begin with those that stand out. **You can always come back to the others later as needed.**

Common Destructive Thought Patterns

Scarcity & Comparison:

- "I don't have enough time."

- "I don't have enough money."

- "There's not enough to go around."

- "Everyone else is ahead of me." / "I'm so far behind."

- "Others are better at this than I am."

Productivity & Worth:

- "If I rest, I'm lazy."

- "I need to prove myself constantly."

- "Being busy means I'm valuable."

Capacity for Change:

- "People don't really change."

- "It's too late for me."

- "If I change, others will reject me."

Relationships & Love:

- "I have to earn love."

- "People will leave me."

- "I need to keep people happy to be safe."

Fear-Based Limitations:

- "If I try, I'll fail."

- "It's safer not to want too much."

- "The unknown is too scary."

Self Criticism & Dismissal:

- "I'm not good enough."

- "There's something wrong with me."

- "I can't trust myself."

These are just some of the belief currents that might run beneath the surface of our decisions, reactions, and sense of possibility. As you continue through this chapter, we'll start exploring how to gently identify, question, and begin shifting the ones that most resonate with your experience. *Remember: seeing clearly is the first move toward choosing freely.*

Reflection:

- Do any of these destructive beliefs resonate with you?

- What do they sound like in your mind?

- Are there other more subtle beliefs that you notice?

- What are the themes spoken by your inner voice?

- Which are the most problematic statements you notice?

- Which are the most supportive?

Let's now begin to walk through some examples of common destructive beliefs in more detail. This isn't to say these beliefs are completely made up, a common example could be someone having less money than they would like. The goal here is to help you investigate if any have become perceived as an absolute truth in your mind. What we want is to keep ourselves from forming rigid beliefs that don't hold any space for the contradiction that would be necessary to start changing or expanding beyond them.

Scarcity & Comparison

People Can't Change

You might think, "It's impossible to change; we're hard wired the way we are". Sure, there may be some ways in which we stay "as-is", but we are much more adaptable than we used to think. The nature vs. nurture model doesn't take into account something very important: free will.

You may think "if I change, I'll just revert back later," but that depends on a lot of things, including but not limited to:

1. How important the change is to you

2. How long you've been practicing the new lifestyle

3. Whether or not you update your beliefs

You may also think, "it's easier for other people to change than it is for me," but while it may seem that way it's actually really difficult for most people to change. Change isn't easy, and it's not supposed to be, but you can make it easier by being completely invested in it. This way you are not wasting your energy internally fighting the change half the time. The best way you can do that is by recognizing how important the change is to you and *why*.

For example, someone who has celiac disease needs to not eat gluten to keep their body from going into an autoimmune state (e.g., the body attacking its own cells, which can lead to all sorts of comorbidities). If that person knows without a doubt that they aren't going to cheat on their diet, then it's not a struggle anymore. It's just then about figuring out how to change their lifestyle and making sure to have other foods available to eat. When you make an important change like this as a foundational decision, you can then redirect all of your energy involved with the change toward the technical details of how to do it. Rather than spending 10, 20, 50, 80% of the energy involved on deciding *if* you are going to do it that day, you can spend 100% on *how*. It might not be easy, but it's already been decided.

I Don't Have Enough Time

This is one of the most universal beliefs. It's one that quietly governs our priorities, stress levels, and sense of possibility. You might think, "I just can't find the time to make this change right now." On the surface, it seems factual. Life feels full. There are obligations, people to care for, and responsibilities that feel non-negotiable. But underneath the surface, focusing on this belief can also serve as a form of protection. If we're too busy, we're safe from having to face the uncertainty of change...or the discomfort of failure.

The truth is, time doesn't always have to be the gatekeeper. Often, the problem isn't time itself, but how fragmented our focus has become. Many people don't realize how much time is spent passively on things that don't deeply matter, things that they often don't even need or want to do. It feels like just a few minutes but scrolling, worrying, replaying conversations, delaying decisions, but these all add up significantly when compounded. When we begin to clarify what truly matters to us, we often find that there *is* at least some time we can work with. Not endless amounts, but enough to take a step. Even a few minutes moving in a direction that feels meaningful is worthwhile time spent.

Start small. Ten minutes to test something new, five minutes to reflect, or even 60 seconds of focusing on your breath. Choose one thing that brings you closer to your goals, and do it before the day slips away. That action, repeated regularly, can become a bridge off the island of belief that you don't have time. And over time, you'll see that you have far more agency than you once thought. You'll prove to yourself that you can make time for the things that matter. You'll build evidence that you have the ability to utilize your time to its potential, when you allow yourself.

I Don't Have Enough Money

This belief is deeply rooted in our sense of safety, identity, and possibility. It can show up as: "I can't afford to pursue what I want," "I need more money before I can feel secure," or "If I spend money, I'll run out." Money, for many people, becomes a symbolic stand-in for power, permission, and even self-worth.

While it's true that money impacts our options, it's also true that not every internal shift requires financial abundance. Many meaningful changes begin with a shift in mindset, daily habits, and how we treat ourselves rather than a large purchase. Believing that money is the only missing piece can cause paralysis and push us to delay change indefinitely.

If you're feeling stuck here, start by exploring what you *can* access, and what beliefs are hiding under the surface of your relationship with money. Do you feel guilty spending on yourself? Do you equate having more with being more valuable or respectable? What would change if you believed you, yourself, are your most valuable asset?

Even small financial choices can create momentum. For example, you might set aside a few dollars to support a dream, seek free or low-cost resources, or redirect energy from impulse purchases to intentional ones. The point isn't to ignore reality; it's to ask whether this belief is truly fixed, or if it can bend, shift, and gradually open up to something more empowering. When your beliefs shift, sometimes the opportunities you notice do too.

A shift could look like increased creativity regarding how to make more money. People often think of get-rich-quick schemes as either a goal to pursue or something to completely avoid. But what if, instead of looking for a shortcut, you reframed money as a reward for adding value to society? What if you were also optimistic about potential income opportunities and open to brainstorming ways you could enjoy contributing?

What skills can you use to serve others, and which of those skills might lead to sustainable rewards? This could include intellectual, emotional, creative, relational, etc. You don't have to have it all figured out. One small experiment could lead to a fulfilling side hobby, and sometimes those hobbies snowball into entirely new careers and income streams. It's not about the pressure to monetize everything; it's about being open to the creative power of contribution and seeing money as a mechanism and reward. It doesn't have to be mysterious, out of reach, or paired with unchangeable limitations. This openness can inspire creativity and curiosity.

There's Not Enough to Go Around

This belief feeds a sense of competition, comparison, and quiet urgency. It can sound like: "I missed my chance," "someone else already claimed that role," or "if they get ahead, I fall behind." When we believe there's only so much success, love, opportunity, or visibility available, we often shrink ourselves to stay safe or rush toward goals we haven't even decided we want.

This mindset often comes from environments where resources truly did feel scarce emotionally, financially, or socially. It's a survival adaptation, one that helped us stay alert in places where approval or support was conditional or limited. But continuing to live in that state can keep us from seeing collaboration, creativity, and personal timing as legitimate forms of success.

Start gently challenging this belief by looking for examples of abundance: people who lift others as they grow, communities that thrive when individuals flourish, or moments when you have had enough, or maybe even more than you needed. Scarcity might have had a part in shaping you, but it doesn't have to define your future. There is more space, more possibility, and more grace than this old belief would have you think.

As you shift the mindset, you'll start to see more win-win scenarios as you choose to believe they exist. Imagine a small town where five businesses thrive, not by outcompeting each other, but by helping one another. The book store promotes the local coffee shop by hosting author events with their beverages available. The coffee shop features handmade mugs from a local artisan. The artisan sources materials from the nearby general store. The general store recommends customers grab lunch from the restaurant next door. And the restaurant gives coupons that lead people back to the book store. When we create together rather than compete from scarcity, our efforts become exponential. We rise together and our abundance grows.

Everyone Else Is Ahead of Me

This belief quietly feeds discouragement, shame, and inertia. It can sound like: "I'm behind", "What's the point in starting now?", or "I should have figured this out by now." The belief assumes there's a timeline you've already failed to meet and that others are all further along on it. But life is not a race, and personal growth isn't a competition. You are not late or behind. You are simply *where you are* and that's the only place you can move forward from. Accepting this gives you power to start moving forward rather than punishing yourself for perceived failure.

This belief often ties into constant exposure to comparison including social media feeds, performance metrics, family expectations, etc. But those glimpses are never the full picture. What looks like someone else's "ahead" may be the middle of their journey or a completely different path. It doesn't take into account your challenges or your other strengths. You can't follow your own timing if you're measuring against someone else's clock.

Reframe your narrative. What if your timeline is perfect for *you*? What if what feels like a detour was actually preparation for depth, clarity, or perseverance that you wouldn't have gained any other way?

It's still important to grow and improve, but trying to get better shouldn't mean slamming yourself for where you are. You have the option to acknowledge and appreciate yourself as you are right now. The present moment is the only one you can affect, so you might as well utilize it to either grow or experience joy, and it's important to actively choose both of those to keep a balance in your life. You are beautiful today, so remember to take time to choose to see your own beauty and feel that love. You are not meant to live someone else's life. You're here to live yours, in your style, choices, and on your own timeline.

Look at what matters most to you right now. Ask: what's one thing I can do today that's aligned with who I want to become? And then do that. That's what being "on time" really looks like.

Others Are Better at This Than I Am

This belief can feel like a quiet weight on your motivation. It tells you not to bother because someone else has already mastered the thing you're just beginning. It might whisper that you'll never catch up, or worse, that trying will just prove how far behind you really are. But this belief ignores one powerful truth: Everyone in a place of mastery was once a novice. The willingness to do it anyway should be valued.

Everyone starts somewhere. The people you admire once struggled to begin, too. And even now, no one is good at everything. People have strengths, yes, but they also have blind spots, limitations, and entire areas they haven't explored. You might be new to something they're fluent in, but you're also likely fluent in something they've never even touched.

Let's say, hypothetically, it's true that someone else is ahead of you in one area. For example, if you want to be more fit and they've been doing calisthenics for five years. Sure, they might be stronger than you physically. But maybe emotionally, you are deeply mature and compassionate, while they might be struggling in their relationships. You wouldn't know. You can't compare comprehensively, so it's not really a fair comparison. Comparison can help us clarify our goals or even motivate us, but it should never be used to put ourselves down.

Skill is not identity. Talent is not superiority. You are not less valuable because someone else is further along in a particular area. If anything, your willingness to begin is a strength they may have forgotten. Even if they do understand this value and implement it well, then great, you should add it to your toolbelt as well.

Try shifting from comparison to curiosity. Instead of "they're better than me," ask "what can I learn here?" or "how can this inspire my own growth?" Let it motivate, not diminish you. And remember, the only fair comparison is between who you are now and who you're becoming.

Productivity & Worth

The destructive beliefs that can occur in this category generally assume that your value is conditional: based on output, visible effort, or constant momentum. But rest is not laziness. It is recovery, reflection, and recalibration. In fact, allowing time for intentional rest is often the very thing that allows us to contribute with greater creativity and depth.

The pressure to prove yourself constantly can mask a deeper fear: that without doing more, you are *not enough*. Your worth isn't something you earn, it's something you carry by being alive, conscious, authentically yourself, and exercising love and compassion. There's nothing inherently wrong with ambition or drive, but if your productivity becomes your identity, then your sense of worth becomes fragile.

While being busy might feel validating, busyness isn't the same as purpose. Sometimes we stay busy to avoid discomfort. Sometimes it's out of habit. But staying busy isn't always the best way to move forward. Instead of using productivity as your measuring stick, consider asking yourself: Am I doing what truly matters to me? Is this effort aligned with who I want to be and how I want to live?

Value doesn't come from activity alone. It comes from presence, integrity, intention, and alignment. You are not a machine, nor do you have to perform like one. You are a human being and inherently valuable, even on your quietest day.

Beliefs About Change

These beliefs carry a heavy emotional charge because they speak to our identities, certainty, and the fear of instability. Believing that change is impossible keeps us trapped not because it's true, but because it becomes a self-fulfilling prophecy. People *do* change, sometimes dramatically, but usually through small and consistent shifts. Change doesn't require perfection. It requires decisiveness and repetition.

The belief that it's too late implies that transformation has an expiration date. But many of the world's most meaningful shifts happen after detours, setbacks, or long periods of waiting. The question isn't "Is it too late?" It's "What do I want to do with the time I have now?"

Fearing that others will reject you if you change is natural. Some people may resist or misunderstand your growth, especially if they benefitted from your former patterns. But that's not a reason to stay small. True connection can withstand evolution, and new connections often appear as you become more aligned. You don't have to overhaul your life overnight. You just need to be willing to meet yourself honestly, and keep taking steps one moment, one choice at a time.

Relationships & Love

Relationships are the landscape where many of our core beliefs come into play. Whether romantic, familial, or social, if you find yourself thinking, "I have to earn love", "People will leave me", or "I need to keep people happy to be safe" you're not alone. These beliefs often grow out of early relational dynamics where love, attention, or safety felt conditional.

When we internalize the message that we have to perform or sacrifice ourselves to receive love, it can create patterns of people-pleasing or emotional withdrawal. These responses can even lead to excessive selflessness or selfishness, causing one to take too much responsibility for others (e.g. compulsive empathy), or not enough responsibility for themselves (e.g. narcissistic tendencies). These responses often kept us safe in the past, but today, they may be keeping us disconnected from the very closeness we long for.

Love built on true connection is not earned, it's given. People can love you because of your presence, not just your performance. Those who require you to abandon yourself to be "loved" are offering conditional relationships, not care. It can feel risky to change these patterns, especially when they've been your "normal." But healing begins by noticing when these beliefs surface and asking challenging but deeply impactful questions.

Reflection:

- What would love look like if I felt safe to be myself?

- What would connection feel like without chasing it?

- How can conflicts be discussed with mutual respect?

- If I love myself consistently, without condition, does approval from others become less important?

- How can I show up for myself and others with less conditions?

- How do I love more unconditionally while maintaining healthy boundaries?

Stay connected to your truth while leaving room for others to do the same. That is the beginning of real love and the beginning of healthier relationships of every kind.

I'm not suggesting you cut out all the people in your life who are offering conditional love. In some cases it might be appropriate, we often maintain many different types of relationships in our lives. After all, we're all doing our best with what we currently have to offer; it's also very hard to be truly unconditional in our love. Some boundaries are healthy, but they should consider both people's needs. In some cases, you might be accepting people in your life as they are, with a new perspective on how to hold space for that person. In others, it might mean shifting the boundaries or letting go of the relationship. It could even mean helping someone else see new ways of being through your own shifting. You can't decide for someone else, but you can communicate with them and offer them the ability to heal and grow with you, if they choose.

Fear-Based Limitations

Fear-based beliefs are often coming from a place of being protective at their core, but are also profoundly limiting. They usually arise in moments of uncertainty, disappointment, or being challenged, and they're designed to keep you safe from the possibility of pain.

The fear of failure can convince you not to try, yet trying without guarantee of success is the only path to progress. Often what we call "failure" is simply a step along the learning curve. There is wisdom in caution, but if caution becomes a cage, it's time to reassess. Perhaps instead of only seeing effort as resulting in "Success" and "Failure," our mental model could look more like:

Inaction	Action
Disengage → Apathy	Fail → Learn → Succeed → Achieve

Ignoring your aspirations, in order to also avoid disappointment, is another common approach. But numbing your desires doesn't make them disappear, it just silences the very voice that can guide you toward growth, joy, and meaning. Wanting something doesn't make you greedy or unrealistic, assuming you aren't harming others in the process of chasing it. It makes you human and shows that you are experiencing one of the coolest things about us, our ability to express creativity.

And as for the fear of the unknown, it's real. But it's also where transformation happens. Staying where you are may feel safer, but it's not the same as being satisfied. The unknown is not always dangerous. And the known doesn't really guarantee safety or certainty. Being willing to face unknowns at the right time, leads us to where the best opportunities live. The healing, the possibility, the version of you that you've never met before.

You don't have to rush into risk, but be allowed to take them when they are calculated and feel right for you. Let fear be a signal, not a stop sign. It might not be a cliff, it could be the edge of your next breakthrough.

Reflection:

- Are there any fears that are holding you back?

- If you wanted to take a small brave step into a new possibility, what would it be?

- Are there any risks you feel unable to take, even though you really want to?

- What **exactly** is holding you back?

- What happens if you try to think of creative solutions to current challenges?

Self Criticism & Dismissal

Self-critical beliefs are often the quietest yet most constant inner voices. They are the ones that may say, "I'm not good enough", "There's something wrong with me", or "I can't trust myself." They can become so deeply embedded in our thinking that we mistake them for fact, or don't even hear them at all. They might be camouflaged in the details of the stories we repeat to ourselves. If we let them end up becoming subtle assumptions in our minds, ones that our self-talk actually operates a layer above, they can become more difficult to notice and shift. But when looking more closely at our thoughts and listening carefully, we can see the core of their motives and start to address any self-dismissal.

This kind of inner dialogue often stems from childhood experiences, cultural narratives, or moments when we were deeply hurt or misunderstood. Over time, self-protection turned into self-rejection. The mind tries to keep us from disappointment by keeping us from adequately valuing ourselves, and in doing so, also keeps us from our potential.

The truth is, no one is perfect. No one is exempt from mistakes, fear, or doubt. But you don't have to treat your flaws as facts or your fears as final. You can learn to trust yourself by choosing small, self-honoring actions and witnessing your own follow-through. You can also witness yourself recovering from let downs and moving forward, proving that you can start to trust yourself. If your inner voice constantly criticizes or dismisses you, it's time to start noticing it and questioning it.

Healing doesn't mean you never doubt yourself. It means that when doubt arises, you meet it with curiosity, self-compassion, and a growing belief that you are worth rooting for.

Reflection:

- Are there any moments where you brush past your own needs, dismiss compliments, or talk down to yourself?

- What kinds of things do you say to yourself when you make a mistake?

- Do you recognize any patterns in your inner voice that feel limiting, harsh, or unkind?

- How might you be able to add in some more uplifting self-talk in those moments?

- What positive things could you tell yourself that you can resonate with?

- What would help shift your attention to a more supportive and hopeful state?

Chapter Summary

If you've made it through this chapter, you've done something courageous. You've taken time to look inward not with judgment, but with curiosity. You've begun to investigate what has quietly shaped your behavior including your beliefs and self-talk. Even if the specific examples in this book didn't feel relatable, you've still been practicing opening your mind to look for these types of habitual and impactful thought trends. Perhaps you have noticed there are other personal beliefs you would like to better understand; ones that are more specific to your experiences and life. You can take this practice forward into investigating those as well.

From here, our focus will begin to shift. We will move from clarifying what old limiting or destructive beliefs have been holding you back, to building what can move you forward: new creative beliefs. What you do next will depend on what you value most. And the good news is, you get to decide.

Chapter 3: Shifting Your Focus

Focusing on what you dislike can sharpen your awareness, but stay there too long, and you'll reinforce the very thing you want to leave behind. This chapter is about changing your relationship with focus. Instead of fueling your resistance, you'll learn how to redirect your energy toward what you want to grow. It's like trying to escape a shadow by staring at it. Instead, only notice the gap areas. Then shift your focus to what you want to grow, like you would if you were tending a plant. What you water will grow.

Even your critics should serve your vision, not distract you from it. Investigate what they tell you. Ask yourself whether there's any truth or insight to be gained, even if the message wasn't delivered kindly. If so, reshape it into something that motivates you with kindness to carry forward. Even unhelpful feedback can offer something valuable when viewed through the lens of your growth. For example, if someone told you a book you were writing is confusing, you could investigate whether there are areas you could be more *clear*. Clarity becomes the focus, and the criticism is let go. As you trust that you learned what you needed from it, it can simply drift away like a twig in a stream.

Transforming Through Pain

Yes you probably have trauma, as do I. So does the barista who made your coffee, and the nurse who changed your IV. This work isn't intended to crown ourselves as king or queen of the broken. It's to gather the wisdom that came from it, honor the pain, and then keep walking. We face our trauma *not to live in it*, but to deepen our wisdom.

Part of that wisdom also leads us back to clearing the way for joy, purpose, and love. The transformation isn't about glorifying the wound; it's about using what we've learned to walk forward with decisiveness and strength. Healing becomes not the goal, but the byproduct of alignment with what matters most. When trauma is acknowledged with curiosity rather than attachment, it can help illuminate our path forward.

Acknowledging pain matters. Speaking our challenges out loud has real value, whether it's with someone else or just with ourselves. Having someone else hear us and understand how we felt can profoundly assist us in choosing, and being ready, to move forward. Even sitting by ourselves and saying out loud, "I felt this way when this happened" or "this experience hurt", can be cathartic.

It's important to recognize the healing nature of this process and also to see that we need to be honest with ourselves about the intent. If reflecting becomes the recurring reliving of the past, it crosses the line of being a healthy exercise and becomes a trend. We don't want to create patterns where we are reinforcing the experience as a "common pathway" for our minds. Honest reflection can help us assess when it's time to vent, feel, or dig deeper towards understanding, and when it's time to shift our focus to something new.

Reflection:

- What have you been trying *not* to do or think about?

- What could you learn through willingly facing it?

- What would it look like to redirect instead of resist?

- What past experiences do you commonly focus on?

- What might be a healthy, forward-moving focus you could practice in its place?

- Are there habits, thoughts, or patterns that could be replaced with something more aligned with your life?

Shifting Focus and Expanding Potential

Before moving forward, it may help to ask yourself: What is the ratio of destructive to constructive beliefs in my daily thinking? You don't have to criticize yourself if the answer is not what you want, just notice. Are most of your thoughts helping you grow, or holding you back? Does your current ratio change in different areas of your life (work, relationships, goals, etc.)? The goal isn't perfection. It's recalibration. Even shifting the ratio slightly in favor of growth-supporting beliefs can create profound changes over time.

You can't actively **not** do something. Rather than striving to avoid what we don't want, it serves us to focus on how to replace it. For example, if you're trying to stop scrolling on your phone every night before bed, it's much harder to simply "not scroll" than it is to replace that habit with reading a few pages of a book or stretching for five minutes. Your mind and body need something to move toward, not just something to resist.

I'm not doing a lot of things while I write this (e.g. I'm not eating, at a party, or riding a horse) but that doesn't mean I need to focus on all the things I'm not doing. In fact, can you see how trying to think of all the things I'm not doing would burn up energy that could otherwise be used focusing on what I intend to be doing (i.e. writing this book)? Energy flows toward action. When you obsess about what you don't want, you feed that version of reality, or at the very least, starve what you actually want. Instead, point your willpower toward what you **do** want. That's where transformation lives.

What you focus on becomes your reality. What you think about reiteratively becomes easy for your brain to think about, and therefore what it thinks about more readily on its own when in autopilot. This in turn changes what you do, say, and the actions you take. Your focus downstream becomes what you do, and eventually, who you are. While we are working in the current, we are also shifting it for our future selves. This creates the life you lead. This is because your mind is automatically taking care of a lot of things for you, all the time. What you feed into your repeated thoughts directly impacts the outcomes of your life, and the lines are very blurred between input and output.

The downside to our mental autopilot capabilities is that sometimes we become numb to some of these trends. It happens so quickly, we don't always notice what we are doing. But becoming aware of this process is very empowering. You can start intentionally building a practice of adding inputs that will shape your life in positive ways you won't have to actively pursue in the future. This is the upside of your brain's automatic patterns. Building a new focus takes work, and while living by this practice can require some ongoing effort, it pays you back exponentially. The more effort you put in, the more the results you are seeking will become natural and lead to new potentialities. You may be surprised to find out who you can become and what you can achieve.

Reflection:

- What is something you would like to focus more energy on this week?

- What small action could you take today, to shift your focus in that direction?

- What is a larger goal you want to set your sights on?

- How could you align a few more steps in that direction in the near-term?

Building a Practice

As you begin to shift your energy toward something new, it helps to identify how you want your daily practice around that focus to look. This doesn't need to be rigid or complicated. It just needs to be consistent and chosen by you. This supports you to better stay in alignment with your hopes, rather than falling back into your learned habits. The beginning of a practice could be as simple as journaling for five minutes each morning about your intention, visualizing your current goal before bed, or writing your focus word on a sticky note where you will see it often. It could even be practiced primarily in your mind, just catching old beliefs when they happen and saying a new positive one to yourself a few times. You're not trying to force change; you're building a pattern with your attention. The more consistently you water a plant the more likely it will survive and thrive. The more you spend time on your new focus, the more naturally it will grow. As it grows, it becomes easier to maintain and you will gain reserves to tackle additional challenges or reach for higher goals.

Replacement Strategies and Techniques

When you notice an old pattern or limiting habit emerging, that's a cue. Not to judge yourself, but to redirect your energy. It can help when times are tough to have a few go-to replacement strategies ready. Making time for reflections when you aren't feeling triggered is also important. It's easier to get a deeper understanding and be forward thinking when life is flowing more smoothly. It's important to practice both. Let's walk through a few example ideas you can reference and expand on, or you can entirely design your own:

- Swap a negative thought with a question:

  - *What's another way to look at this?*

- Investigate the negative thought, then fill the gap:

  - *"Why am I being so hard on myself right now?", "Oh I'm feeling afraid of failing again."*

  - Replace with: *"My new model for failures is different. Failures are stepping stones towards more successes, and eventually achieving goals."*

- When your state is not what you want (sad, worried, etc.) for an extended period of time, you can try practicing a grounding exercise.
    - Go for a walk outside
    - Have a hot cup of tea
    - Try a meditation focused on feeling sensations from your environment
- Journal out about your beliefs and replacements as needed. You can even ask additional questions in your reflections journal such as:
    - *What thoughts were repetitive today?*
    - *Were these thoughts supporting me? If not, how do I choose to shift them?*
- Take a few moments of quiet time:
    - Learn to accept some silence in your life and give yourself permission to not be "doing something".
    - Relax, rest your eyes, or do a calming activity. Choose whatever feels right to you.
- Speak aloud a new affirmation or intention:
    - The more you say it, the easier it will be to connect with it and feel truth in it.
    - Notice as you practice an affirmation you would like to feel true, is the meaning shifting over time?
    - You can be open to changing the affirmation to one that feels more aligned as needed, but practicing

will help you keep your focus on the goal as you find the best fit for you.

- Use **6-way breathing**:
  - Inhale deeply and slowly while expanding your lungs down as far as you can in your torso,
  - Expand your sides, back, and belly allowing the breath to rise all the way up. Like filling a balloon.
  - When you exhale, do it slowly and fully following the same order (down, out, up).
  - Repeat 6 breaths, or for a few minutes if you're feeling up to it. This calms your nervous system, re-centers your focus, and helps restore connections in the mind and body.

What matters most is that you have a few supportive options when you catch yourself slipping into patterns that no longer serve you.

Reflection:

- What do you want your practice to look like?

- What is the optimized version you want to work towards?

- What is the first habit you are going to add to your practice immediately?

- What other habits do you want to add in the near-term?

- What support system can you put in place to make these changes easier to experiment with and maintain?

Future-Self Vision Prompt

Your future self already exists as a possibility. The more clearly you can see this version of you, the easier it becomes to move toward and create this reality. Take a quiet moment and visualize yourself five years from now. Not the version shaped by fear or expectation. The version shaped by love, alignment, and intention.

<u>Reflection:</u>

- Where are you?

- What do your days feel like?

- How do you speak to yourself?

- What choices have become easy?

- What have you released?

- What lights you up?

- What are the most meaningful impacts resulting from the changes you've made?

This future version of you is not a fantasy. It's a possible outcome of your focus, your attention, and your willingness to stay committed to the process of healing and growth.

Chapter Summary

Redirecting your attention is not about ignoring your problems. It's about practicing sovereignty over your energy. Where your focus goes, your life flows. When you shine light on the right places, wisdom becomes inevitable. That wisdom helps to best align your goals and purpose. Then what you shower with your attention, will flourish.

Focus is not about force, it's about nurturing. This means showing up for your vision every day, in small ways, until it becomes real. It may feel uncertain at times to keep moving toward what you want to believe in, when you don't have proof it will be there. It may feel risky to put energy into something before it has fully taken form. This means leaning into the discomfort of uncertainty, which is something you can absolutely do, if you choose to. That willingness and quiet persistence is how transformation begins. You are capable through decision and devotion.

Part II:

Creating Your Compass

Chapter 4: Moments Become Momentum

Maintaining Progress

At this point, you might be feeling a surge of motivation, a sense of overwhelm, or a general feeling of momentum. These feelings can be energizing, and they can feel unsteady, like trying to stand up against waves in the ocean. You could be wondering how to keep that momentum going. Maybe you've had experiences in the past where you felt this way, and then the energy quickly burned up. Then later, you felt like you were dragging. Here's a little secret to take with you on your journey: you don't have to do it all at once. In fact, you probably can't. Some decisions are huge and pivotal and change you forever from that day forward, it really can happen that way. But that's not the standard for how change usually happens. Instead, most change happens incrementally, through practicing new habits paired with a strong enough *why* to keep going when it's hard.

One thing that will help you is remembering to incorporate balance when you find space, generally anytime you are feeling an extreme. You can breathe and take it easy even when you're feeling a ton of motivation, in order to conserve some energy. You can also push even when you don't feel like you have gas in the tank. It's possible to find some energy to move forward, even when we're *feeling* unmotivated.

You don't grow the plant, you tend the soil. You water. You prune. You create the conditions. Growing yourself is no different. It's not a matter of *fixing* yourself; it's about doing what needs to be done so your body, mind, and heart can do what they already know how to do: *heal, expand, and experience joy.*

Reflection:

- What has gotten in the way of your progress before?

- What modifications could you make to your beliefs to keep you on course when your momentum is challenged?

- What are some things you could choose in any individual moment to build a little momentum?

- How would that impact your life over time?

Do What You Can

There will be days when you don't feel inspired. Motivation may feel miles away. You might feel foggy, heavy, uncertain, overwhelmed, or just generally tired. That's not a failure. It's part of being human. Everyone has up days and down days. But those are the moments where something powerful can happen: you can show up anyway. You can commit to giving it whatever you can muster today, rather than waiting for optimal conditions. That is something not everyone does, it's something special.

When motivation is low, the habit of showing up matters more than the feeling. Even if you don't get nearly as much done as you would on a more motivated day, it's still progress. It's not about going hard all the time, it's about going at all. Walking for five minutes. Researching for ten minutes. These tiny movements prove something to your subconscious: you are becoming a person who keeps promises to yourself. It also means that going for it anyway helps train your mind to associate follow-through with ease, and over time, it will cost you less energy as the pattern becomes familiar and self-reinforcing.

Discipline when grounded in self-respect and purpose, rather than criticism and pressure, can be the bridge between who you were and who you want to become. It doesn't have to feel like a grind. It can feel like a gift. You're not forcing yourself, you're supporting yourself by showing yourself consistency in what you've decided to do.

Try saying something like this to yourself, and notice the impact: "I don't have to feel like it. I can start anyway." I don't want to promote that everyone always has to hustle, but discipline is an important and worthwhile skill to cultivate. Just remember to practice honesty with yourself about when you actually need rest, and when you will feel better if you push yourself to proceed.

Reflection:

- What's one area of your life where you tend to wait for motivation before acting?

- What would "doing it anyway" look like, including gentleness and self-respect?

- Do you find yourself never allowing adequate rest?

- What if you rested enough to refill the tanks before proceeding?

- How well are you listening to your body and mind? How could you improve?

Building Motivation Daily

Motivation is often misunderstood. We wait for it like the weather. Hoping it shows up, disappointed when it doesn't. But in reality, motivation is more like a muscle. It grows when you use it. This can hurt at first, especially if you've been sedentary for a while. But, it will build more than you might be able to visualize right now. You just need to get started today to see the results compounded in the future.

Think of it like lighting a fire. You don't wait for warmth before striking the match. Action is the spark. Even the smallest forward movement can generate just enough internal shift to make the next step easier. That's how motivation builds: through engagement, not waiting to be ready. It will also build faster if you think about how to get leverage from your activities, like adding kindling to a fire. But you don't always have to be the most efficient, just doing something makes for some variation of progress. For example, let's say you start a fire the hardest way possible: with two sticks. It takes you all day, but at least you are getting stronger and more skilled at fire making. Sometimes doing things the hard way teaches us how to get more leverage in the future, or at the very least, helps us appreciate it more when we get there.

Daily motivation isn't about grand declarations. It's about creating small moments of momentum. Stretching in the morning. Choosing the nourishing meal. Saying the encouraging thing to yourself. These are seeds. With time, they grow into sustainable drive. Taking these kinds of actions inspires us to take more actions like them. For example, if you exercise you may be more likely to grab a healthier meal, and vice versa. If you say "hi" to a stranger, you are more likely to have an interesting conversation with them or someone else later in the day.

The key is making space for these small victories. A daily practice: whether it's a checklist, a journal prompt, some kind of ritual, or just an internal dialog saying "nice, you did it!", can reinforce that you're building something. You're not waiting to become the kind of person who shows up. You already are, you're just in the process of getting better at it. You're not waiting to give yourself permission to be the person you want to be. You're doing it today, little by little, and thus making it more natural to be that person one action at a time.

Reflection:

- What intentional action could you take each morning?

- What about before bed?

- What habits could you build into your daily activities?

- How could you celebrate or acknowledge these efforts?

- What would most deeply strengthen your willpower?

Sustaining Momentum

Motivation that lasts isn't loud. It's not about being hyped all the time, it's about being aligned and dedicated. Life will ebb and flow. Your energy will shift. But if you're anchored to your deeper "why," you can ride those waves without getting pulled under.

Long-term motivation is less about passion and more about orientation. You don't need to feel excited every day. You have permission to do a little exploring and maybe even get a little disoriented for a moment. You're allowed to take a pause and relax. You just need to know which direction you're headed and keep getting back on track. Always moving towards what you want. Sometimes that means stopping for a break. Sometimes that means recommitting. You're taking steps, and those steps add up when you keep calibrating yourself towards the right direction.

Remind yourself often what this is for, and where you are headed. That clarity is what keeps you steady. Knowing your intention and feeling connected to a purpose calls you back to your path. Training your will power to grow and support you through your journey.

Reflection:

- Why did I begin this journey?

- Where am I going?

- What do I care about?

- What am I building?

- What is my core motivation for the changes I'm making? What is my "why"?

Relaxing Into Progress

Progress doesn't require extensive pressure. In fact, the idea that growth has to be intense is one of the biggest reasons people quit. If you don't find balance, it can burn you out before the benefits have time to show. It costs a lot of mental energy to experience stress. What if you replaced that habit with a belief that you don't have to feel stressed to get it done? What if you trusted that you will move forward and allowed yourself to do it from a place of peace? It might take time to fully believe it, but those are ideas you can start to reinforce and build as a part of your updated mindset.

You're allowed to move forward gently. You're allowed to pause, breathe, reset, and begin again without shame. Let progress feel like a quest, not a race. When you soften your grip, you make space for your natural creativity and energy to re-enter the process. Intuition can have a hard time reaching us while our minds are overflowing with repeated thoughts and feelings. Making space can quickly pay off when it comes to meaningful progress.

Sometimes the most productive thing you can do is rest. Or laugh. Or take a step back to see the bigger picture. Growth happens when the environment is nurturing, far more than when the process is rushed. Just as we don't yank on a seedling to make it grow faster, we can't force ourselves to transform on command. Instead, we prepare the soil or in this case our mindset, our beliefs, and our actions; we let the process unfold at its natural pace. Balance is sustainable and means we can build and retain more resources internally and externally. Consistency with softness, dedication with rest, commitment with calm, all help restore balance in our lives. This approach generally creates more space for transformation than forced effort alone can, especially when applied over time.

Consider this as a new mantra:
I can make progress in peace. I do not force; I flow.

Reflection:

- Where could you soften your grip and still make progress?

- Are there areas you've been forcing certain outcomes?

- What would it feel like or look like, to nurture growth instead?

- Is there room for more restoration in your habits?

- How often are you breathing deeply and slowly?

Momentum Mindset Shifts

Your mindset is your steering wheel. Small adjustments can drastically alter the direction you're headed over time.

- **Trade intensity for consistency:** Intensity burns fast; consistency builds resilience and momentum.

- **Trade self-criticism for curiosity:** You don't have to antagonize your way into progress. Gentle observation, paired with commitment and compassion, invites lasting change.

- **Trade your perceived ideal pace for sustainability:** Your progress doesn't have to align to anyone else's timeline. The best pace is the one you can keep.

These aren't just affirmations, they're shifts in posture. Practice them daily, and you'll notice that what once felt like a grind begins to feel like grounded movement. Not frantic or fragile. Just real, steady change.

Reflection:

- Do these mindset shifts resonate with you?

- To support balance, do you need more discipline or relaxation?

- How do these ideas apply in different areas of your life?

- Where can you see these shifts helping you the most?

Chapter Summary

In this chapter, we explored how momentum doesn't require constant availability of motivation, it's about consistency and intention. Wisdom can shape what we want to do at the core, leading to more natural actions with less effort required. We shifted from chasing to cultivating motivation.

We also examined how small daily actions, especially when rooted in your deeper "why," can generate more sustainable drive than waiting for bursts of inspiration. Through strategies for low-motivation days, daily motivation building, long-term alignment, and permission to rest, this chapter reframed momentum as something we build moment by moment. This momentum then helps us to build what we desire.

Chapter 5: Wading Through Rapids

Negative emotions are indicators of a gap that exists between where we are and where we want to be. We shouldn't fixate on completely eliminating them, because first of all that's not really possible, and secondly that would eliminate crucial feedback we have available to help us grow. In this chapter we will dive into how we can interact with unpleasant emotions in a way that fuels our self-improvement progress.

Experiencing Emotion Like Water

Imagine that the emotions you haven't wanted are simply sitting there waiting to teach you, patient, like a pool of water. Rather than avoiding these difficult emotions, you have the ability to voluntarily wade in and simply let it be there for a little while. Our minds tend to hold onto emotions that we think we need to learn from. The longer we avoid them, the longer they linger and evolve into something more challenging to face later. If you walk into the pool, you can stay there until your mind feels it has been acknowledged. Then, let it drain away, having served its purpose. Remaining is a glimmering pearl of wisdom that you receive for being courageous and strong enough to face your challenges directly.

Let emotions be like waves in the ocean, where you flow up with them and back down. There may be storms rolling in that cause more intense waves. Sometimes it may even feel like they crash over your head. But even then, stillness can be found slightly below that chaotic surf. Emotionally, the same strategy applies. When something difficult rises up in you like sadness, anger, or fear, the surface can feel overwhelming. But what if, instead of thrashing in the same place, you dove inward? What if you went to the bottom of that emotion, let yourself feel the full depth of it, and then pushed back up with a deeper understanding? Rather than these stormy waves crashing onto you, they would go right past you. You'd surface not only calmer, but also with more perspective, ready to take a new breath.

Sometimes emotions can feel like whirlpools; sudden, strong, and capable of pulling you under. But even a whirlpool has a way through. You don't escape it by fighting against the strongest currents. Instead you escape by finding stillness, allowing the current to move you, and spending your energy mindfully to sustain until you, until you can find a path out... or the current weakens on its own. Emotionally, the same strategy applies. You can't always force your way out against the strongest emotions you have, but you can stay grounded long enough to sense where a gentler path is opening up.

Reflection:

- What emotions might need your attention today?

- Are there any emotionally charged thoughts that have been coming up more recently?

- How might it look if you were to interact with them from a place of flowing, like water?

Experiencing Emotion Like Fire

While water helps us understand emotions that ebb and flow, fire speaks to something else: transformation. Fire is heat, energy, and alchemy. Unlike water, which teaches us to flow and release, fire teaches us to stay with intensity long enough to be reshaped by it. When you're truly present with an intense emotion, it's not only something you pass through, it's something that changes you. The rage, the sorrow, the panic that chases you; all of these are forms of emotional fire. If they are acknowledged for their transformational capacity, they can be utilized to move you forward, better than before. If they are buried or reiterated indefinitely, they may only be burning up your energy.

When we let ourselves feel these emotions without repression or avoidance, they have the power to refine us. Fire doesn't just destroy; it also purifies. It can burn away what no longer belongs. Emotional fire, when held with awareness and decisiveness, can help illuminate what matters most, and melt the resistance that's been keeping us stuck.

Much like a blacksmith uses flame to soften metal before reshaping it, emotional heat can soften our rigid identities and beliefs, requiring space for change and creating something new. It's uncomfortable, but it's where some of the most meaningful internal shifts take place.

Don't run from the fire. Don't feed it recklessly. Sit near it. Utilize it carefully. Let it transform you.

- What powerful emotions show up most frequently?

- Is it mostly one, or a range of emotions?

- How could they be utilized to transform you?

Embracing Challenging Emotions

Facing uncomfortable emotions is one of the hardest things we do as humans, and one of the most courageous and rewarding. It takes presence, trust, and a willingness to stay open even when everything in us wants to shut down or try to ignore them. Bravery doesn't mean you're fearless. It means you choose to acknowledge what is real right now, even when it's hard. Here's what that can look like:

1. **Being brave enough to see it.** To name what's not working without judgment. To stop pretending and start observing with honesty.

2. **Being brave enough to feel it.** To allow discomfort to have the space it needs to open yourself to change. To let the pain of the gap between who you are, and who you want to be, rise to the surface. To resist the urge to suppress or numb. To stay open long enough to grow.

3. **Being brave enough to change.** To do something different, even if you're not sure it will work, or happen on the timeline you want. To experiment and practice. To

show up again and again until the new way of being you desire becomes part of who you are.

4. **Being brave enough to live in your truth.** To let the world see the real you. To risk vulnerability. To stay present, not because you're finished healing, but because you believe the journey is worth witnessing in real time. To show the world who you are, without expecting to be validated or comforted. The most authentic self-honoring happens when being yourself is the life you've chosen, and you've chosen it for you.

Bravery, in this context, isn't loud. It's not about pushing through aggressively. It's about remaining on your own two feet while you stand in your truth. It's about continuing to remain true to yourself no matter the response you get from others. It's brave to consider feedback, and choose growth; to help yourself and your ability to support your environment. Balancing listening with unshakable trust in yourself, a trust that rebuilds when challenged or diminished is what creates real transformation.

Emotions As Signals

Emotions don't have to be seen as problems, but as messengers. They point to areas of imbalance and unmet needs, gaps between who we are today and where we want to be; showing us what we aren't doing. This leads us to better understand who we want to be and what we need to do to embody this growth. Each emotion has a purpose. When understood and respected, each offers us a path forward.

Anger Used to Build Kindness & Boundaries

Anger arises when something feels unjust or when boundaries are being crossed. It can signal that a value of ours is being threatened. The energy of anger, when harnessed well, helps us act, speak up, and reestablish balance. Rather than suppressing it, ask: *What is this feeling trying to protect?* You may find that the path forward isn't rage, but grounded kindness reinforced by strong and respectful boundaries. If the anger is toward ourselves, it might mean that we need more boundaries around what we will and won't do in the future. It's an opportunity to strengthen our discernment and commitment to the changes we seek in ourselves.

Hate Used to Build Love & Integration

Hate is often the result of deep pain, fear, or prolonged resentment. It forms where understanding has been blocked, a manifestation of separation. It sounds like a strong word. But it can appear in subtle ways that we may not immediately recognize. For example, impatience could be a feeling of hatred towards waiting. The antidote is not denial but integration, recognizing what's being rejected and how it could be accepted. The invitation here is love. Not naive or boundaryless love, but a conscious choice rooted in reconnection with your values. This requires a willingness to replace critical judgment with understanding. Even if we disagree, we can see the beauty that exists in each other, and make space to coexist peacefully.

Worry Used to Build Presence & Trust

Worry comes when our thoughts live in a future we can't control or assume that the difficulties of our past will repeat themselves. It can signal a need for preparation, but if left unmanaged, it robs us of experiencing the present moment. It reflects a gap in trust; maybe in ourselves, in others, or in life as a whole. When worry arises, try anchoring yourself with breath, noticing the environment around you, or creating a ritual you find grounds you back into the now. Building presence helps quiet worry, and choosing to build more trust helps release the illusion of needing full control. We only control ourselves, not the external world. The more we can accept that, the more we can notice and enjoy the gifts available in this moment.

Grief Used to Build Courage & Acceptance

Grief arises from loss and lack and can feel very strong whether real or perceived. It can be from pain that was recent, or long past. However, it is not a weakness. It's a sign that something mattered. Grief, when met honestly, creates space for healing. It's a teacher of what we cherish, what we want, and often, of what we still carry forward. The gap it points to is often between loss, lack, and love, and the bridge across that can be found in both courage and gratitude. The courage to feel, to remember, appreciate, and to rebuild. The ability to see beyond only that we've experienced loss, and practice gratitude for all love we have had the opportunity to receive. The willingness to seek out that which we feel is currently missing from our lives, and to choose to give and receive love despite the possibility of loss.

Fear Used to Build Strength and Will Power

Fear is instinctual. It's a protective signal and a survival mechanism. Without it, we would not sufficiently protect ourselves from harm. But when it becomes chronic or exaggerated, it limits us. Fear can be one of the strongest blockers of progress. But it's also one of the loudest calls to action. It can be a major catalyst to reaching our full potential.

It's important when addressing fear, to discern what is really a threat and what is habitual or an overabundance of caution. When we lean into fear carefully, we often find a strong capacity for direction and movement. And when we act in the face of our fears rather than choosing avoidance, we build true strength. We hone our willpower, understanding, and self-trust, to be able to drive us forward even when fear is activated.

Each emotion tells a story. And when we listen to these signals closely, they also offer us blueprints. They serve us not just for healing pain, but for building the person we're becoming.

Reflection

- Which of these emotions do you experience most often?

- What might emotions be communicating or helping to identify?

- What have you previously tried when responding to this emotion?

- Do you ever find yourself suppressing it, reacting to it, or feeding into it?

- How might you try responding next time?

- What value, trait, or habit could you strengthen by utilizing these emotions constructively?

Emotional Awareness Integration Practice:

It's one thing to understand emotions while reading in a calm moment. It's another to remember their purpose in the middle of a hectic one. That's why integration and practice is so important, so we can get better at this. Try these practices to carry emotional awareness into your daily life:

- **Name emotions in real-time:** Practice saying to yourself, "I feel angry," or "I feel sad", naming it not for judgment but for awareness and acknowledgement.

- **Track emotional triggers:** Notice when an emotion shows up. Is it tied to a specific situation, thought, or belief? Ask things like: "Where did this emotion come from?"

- **Journal reflections:** Each evening or weekly, reflect on what emotion showed up most, what it revealed, and what you might build from it.

- **Create visual anchors:** Use a word, symbol, or image to remind you what you want to build when that emotion visits you again. Or create a reminder that the process of facing these emotions directly is making you stronger, wiser, and more courageous.

Chapter Summary

Emotions are not disruptions to be suppressed. They are messengers. They can be utilized by us as tools, if we choose to be the architects of our own minds. When met with presence and respect, emotions help shape us into healthier and more insightful versions of ourselves.

Through the metaphors of water and fire, we learned that emotions can rise and fall and are meant to transform us, but this only works when we engage with them mindfully. And by understanding the messages of anger, hate, worry, grief, and fear, we gain the opportunity not just to feel, but to *create*.

The furnace of feeling doesn't burn us down. It refines us.

You are not wrong for feeling deeply. It means you care about something enough to feel. You are not being broken by your emotions, you are being reshaped.

Chapter 6: Designing Your Compass

In the chapters before this, we looked at how the "current" is involved in shaping your life. We also investigated how to shift your focus and work within your existing environment to build new momentum. Now it's time to further define your **internal compass**: the core values, inner truths, and steady guidance systems that will help you move through life's inevitable uncertainties with clarity and intention. This tool ensures that you know which direction you're going and allows you to plot your course. Despite existing "currents" and downstream challenges, you are able to continually navigate towards what you want.

A compass doesn't show you every step of the path. It doesn't tell you exactly what to do at all times, but it helps you stay oriented while you explore. It keeps you on your intended path. The compass is something you always return to when you feel lost and can keep you from getting lost in the first place when used correctly.

The Importance of a Compass

Your perspective defines what you see, and what you see reshapes your perspective. It's a feedback loop that can often feel like a closed system, unless we challenge it to expand. When you choose to believe growth is possible, your mind starts to look for openings. When you believe nothing works, you miss the lever right in front of you. Building your compass begins with choosing what lens you'll look through. It continues by increasing curiosity and dedication to your practices.

You might already have rules for yourself that you live life by. We all should. This chapter invites you to revisit them, to see how functional they are as is. Identify whether they should be refined, adapted, or expanded on. It will encourage you to choose various meaningful and sometimes challenging values, even if that means you have to push yourself to become better able to live by them.

Reflection:

- Do you currently connect to certain principles, values, and guidelines for life?

- What are they currently, how quickly do they come to mind?

- Which ones stand out as your top priorities?

- How do you feel about your current consistency with them?

- In what areas could you make improvements?

Your Inner Truth

Your compass begins with **what matters most to you**, you're true north. These aren't things someone else can just give you. They can be inspired or taught by others, but these are the values, ideals, or felt truths that light something up inside you. If you've ever made a choice that felt right, where it required no explanation, then you've touched that inner truth. Someone else can guide you to finding them, or model them to you, but choosing them is up to you.

Reflection:

- What do I care most about?

- When do I feel most alive?

- What do I admire in others?

- What fills my heart?

- What brings me peace?

- What brings me childlike joy?

These are just some ideas to help you find the path back to your internal north. You can change them, expand on them, or be inspired to take other routes to find your answer. Connecting to what resonates with you is a deeply personal question, and unique experience. As you make space for your conscious mind to become aware of your most fundamental truths, they will become stronger and more readily available when you need them. Through this clarity, you also become more responsible to live by them and thus become more of who you are at your core. The real you rises closer to the surface. When you're grounded in finding answers you really deeply believe, you can navigate almost anything.

Compass vs. Current

A compass doesn't prevent you from being pulled by the current, but it helps you notice when you are. When your life starts to feel like it's happening *to* you rather than *for* you; it may be a sign you've lost contact with your internal direction. Life is always in some ways being shaped by you. When it's not going where you want, you will get more from focusing on what you do want to create than becoming apathetic or focusing on resisting what you don't like.

By contrast when you act from your compass, even when you're unsure, you start to feel agency again. Your choices may be small, but they feel aligned. Each one deepens your sense of coherence and purpose. Rather than drifting aimlessly, or fighting to tread water just to stay in the same spot, you will be doing what it takes to go somewhere meaningful.

It doesn't mean there won't be a current pulling and pushing you. Instead, it means that with all of the emotional, habitual, relational, and environmental factors, you will still know where you are headed. When challenges come up, you will find a way to face them.

Knowing where we're going also gives us motivation to find the energy, and the will, to swim through strong currents. Why exhaust yourself if there's no point? But if you have something worth striving for, you can persevere. In the same conditions a heavy weight can feel lighter; a strong current can feel weaker. Not necessarily because it is, but because you and your will have become stronger.

Building Directional Habits

Your compass improves through your practice of paying attention to it. Not by perfectly following it every second, but by returning to it over and over again. You can build habits that act like miniature calibration tools, to check in with your values. This could include journaling, reflecting on your principles before making major decisions, practicing mindfulness even when you're triggered, or saying no when something feels off. These actions allow you to respond with more intention.

Your ability to access and interpret the guidance of your compass improves the more you use it. With enough practice, it can form a voice that you start to hear or intuitively feel, without even having to pull it out of your pocket. A knowing of what is true to you and an autonomic habit of taking action in accordance with that.

This could start by practicing a deeper level of honesty with someone in your life. At first it might feel awkward, and difficult, to say something you normally wouldn't. It might even cause your environment to change, perhaps they get frustrated with you for acting differently than your normal behavior. People tend to crave honesty, but also want familiarity and certainty. However, if you continue to practice you will get better at finding the words you intend to say. You will start to have less resistance to saying them, getting it out more quickly and effectively. The other person may be able to better hear your message or even adapt their level of honesty in response, but that is up to them. We're always impacting our environment, just as we are impacted by it. But we only get to choose for ourselves.

When the Compass Shifts

Sometimes your sense of direction evolves. What once felt true for you may stop feeling right. That doesn't mean your compass was wrong, it just means you are adapting. We are supposed to evolve over time, this is fundamental in our ability to grow. We even change in different environments, some calling for more of one aspect of our personalities and capabilities, and others calling for a completely separate set of tools and skills. Part of maintaining internal orientation is the willingness to update your compass. The most important feature of making sure it remains functional is applying curiosity and honesty to your commitments.

This also means being compassionate with yourself at times where you realize it needs to change, because you notice something was missing. Instead of thinking "I was wrong," think: *"I'm closer now."* That simple reframe allows your path to remain fluid without making your past self "bad" or "naïve." Part of the growth journey means outgrowing parts of your old self; that's natural.

Everyone who is working on themselves looks back at times and sees a version of themselves doing things they wouldn't support today. It's worthwhile to be understanding towards yourself when this happens. Of course it's important not to make excuses for yourself or hide from the emotions that bubble up. But, it's also important to not invite shame or guilt to linger for long. Remember, emotions are just messengers to help us grow. When one rises it's just here to tell you something. If you carry it around forever, it's only weighing you down at that point. Instead, ask yourself: *Do I feel the lesson was learned in completion?* If the answer is yes, you will also be ready to act on it. At that point, it's time to let the emotions go. If you ask and truly listen, and the answer isn't quite yes yet, you can invite this process to broaden the lesson a bit more and find what you needed. The more you open yourself to learning, the more easily the truth can arise. Being invested in this type of insight seeking can welcome lessons that would otherwise mean making more mistakes and taking more time to learn.

Your Compass Interacting Externally

The compass you utilize should not only meet your own personal needs, but also ripple beyond only you to reflect positivity in the world. Let's look at your compass again, now from the lens of your role in society. Consider how you treat others, and how that in turn impacts you. Your compass has both internal and external impact, so it's important to understand how it shapes you and the environment you are in.

Reflection:

- What values are non-negotiable for you?

- When have you acted from a place of alignment?

- How does your alignment impact those around you?

- Do you sometimes betray your compass?

- How do you feel when others don't follow these standards?

- How do you feel when they do?

When the Compass is Cloudy

Sometimes the compass doesn't point clearly north. It's not that it's broken, it's simply crowded with disruptive ideas and needs to be cleaned. Many of us are carrying beliefs, rules, or expectations that aren't actually ours. They may have come from childhood, school, culture, aspects of our religion, or other people's reactions and preferences; especially those we were dependent on. These internalized scripts sound convincing, but they don't always reflect your own genuine truth. If you are carrying these types of contradictions, it just means you haven't yet given yourself permission to let them go.

Ideas on how you can begin to tell the difference:

- **Internalized scripts feel rigid.** They tend to use language like "should," "have to," or "always." They make you feel stuck, rather than responsible.

- **Your inner truth feels alive.** It may be quieter, or louder, but it often feels expansive, deep, and energizing. Even if they are challenging or scary, they feel real.

If you realize that someone else has pushed a rule or belief towards you and you've adopted it with their intensity, you don't have to completely disown it just because you notice it came from an external source. It could still serve a purpose, but perhaps you don't have to keep it at the same volume and scope in your life. For example, if you learned growing up "*I have to be afraid to spend money on the wrong thing*", and you notice it, you can alter it. Maybe something like: "*I spend money with care, prioritizing what is most valuable to me*". If your compass feels cloudy, pause and polish it.

Reflection:

- Is this belief something I personally relate to?

- Does it serve me in some way, or does it feel true?

- What happens when I follow this idea?

- Are there modifications I would like to make to this belief?

- Is it moving me away from, or towards what I want?

Unlearning false direction and expanding your perspective is part of the journey. In fact, every time you clear away someone else's voice, your own becomes a little clearer and easier to hear. You're not betraying anyone else by choosing your path. You're aligning to the best version of yourself, which results in a better version of you impacting others' lives as well.

Principles to Consider

Okay, I acknowledge I just spent the last section saying not to take on other people's beliefs without question, and I stand by that. Your compass should be designed for *you*. But that doesn't mean we can't learn from others. Sometimes we hear something and it immediately rings true. Not because we were told to believe it, but because something inside us *already did*. Sometimes, hearing it just brings it into our conscious mind and gives us a chance to practice it. This in turn strengthens our mental path back to that internal truth.

Here are a few principles, common across different philosophies, religions, and common wisdom that you could spend time pondering or try expanding in your life and witness the results. Each is followed by a value statement, defining how that principle can serve you, if you choose to more deeply integrate it into your own compass:

1. **Be honest**: Truth clears mental clutter and builds real self-respect. It creates a possibility for connections much deeper than those made foggy by lies, omissions, or even half-truths. It also relieves stress to know those who you are closest to truly know you, at your best and even at your worst.

2. **Practice kindness**: It nurtures your community, lowers defensiveness, and transforms relationships. Being kinder to others even makes it a bit easier to be kind to ourselves.

3. **Honor your responsibilities**: Owning your actions builds self-trust and earns trust from others. It enhances your feelings of self-control and belief in your capabilities. It

also helps you practice discernment in what you commit to, and what is worth saying "no" to. This makes your "yesses" more meaningful.

4. **Act with courage**: Bravery helps you move through fear instead of avoiding it. This gives you more power in choosing what life you create.

5. **Practice patience**: It creates space for better decisions and relieves internal pressure. Patience with others, patience with ourselves, it all makes life more enjoyable moment to moment.

6. **Seek understanding**: Understanding replaces critical judgment with curiosity, and helps create room to resolve conflicts. It builds our capacity to have empathy and compassion, thus increasing the amount of love we can give and experience.

7. **Tend to your health**: Physical well-being supports mental, emotional, and even spiritual resilience and clarity. The way we treat our body compounds over time, and drastically impacts the quality of our life and what we are able to do with it.

8. **Spend your time and money wisely**: Financial stewardship helps create more freedom in your life. Time is often under valued, but it is as important as money. Time can be used to build more funds, which can be used to improve the quality of your life, other lives, and support implementation of your goals and purpose. Beyond that, time can and should be appreciated.

9. **Show gratitude**: Gratitude shifts your awareness to what's good and stabilizes your mood. It improves you

emotionally, physically, and mentally when done as a practice. Showing gratitude can increase experiences of joy for you, and may spread to those around you.

10. **Be generous:** Giving expands your own sense of abundance, connection, and meaning. Practicing any form of philanthropy is one of the best things for us personally, in addition to those it helps. It should be done from a place of fullness, in ways you can also afford. For example, you can get creative with your time, skills, ideas, etc.

Of course, none of these are mandates. They're options you can try, explore, or modify as needed. Each one has stood the test of time as stable and reliable guides.

<u>Reflection</u>:

- Which principles resonate with your compass?

- Are there any you would like to add?

- Which do you already consistently practice?

- Are there any you wish to commit to strengthen?

- Are there any you would like to make more natural?

- Where in your life could you practice these principles?

Chapter Summary

Your compass is not a rigid rulebook, it's a living guide. It is built from your inner truths and honed by intention. It is solidified and followed more naturally by each time you choose to act in alignment with it. It helps you navigate not only through quiet waters, but through storms.

A functional compass doesn't require perfection, only active practice. It invites you to reflect, integrate, and respond meaningfully. It's not just about knowing what matters; it's about listening when it speaks, acting in accordance, and further alteration as needed.

As you continue forward, remember your compass is yours to refine. It's shaped by your values, your actions, and your willingness to evolve. When the path isn't clear, let your compass be your guide. A quiet, steady, reminder of who you are and who you are in the process of transforming into.

Chapter 7: Creating Your Life

Healing isn't about finally marking off a specific checkbox, it's a process that can be prioritized throughout your journey. Like a song you can tune into, one that fills your body and mind. The same is true of choosing your life. It's not a one-time decision. It's something you do again and again, not because you failed the first time, but because you are *working on becoming* more of who you truly are. Because different phases are meant to exist in your life, like different chapters in a book. The character doesn't start fully optimized, they grow along the way.

You don't need to be perfect. You need to develop the right ratios to reflect your goals profoundly in your life. The question doesn't need to be: "Did I fail today?" Instead it could be: "Did I nurture myself often enough to grow?" or "Did I focus on the right things, to have them occur more abundantly in my life?"

<u>Reflection</u>:

- Did your new intentions outweigh your old habits today?

- What old habits did you notice occurring?

- How do you want to approach them when they appear?

- What new tendencies are you building to replace them?

- Are you satisfied with the attention you put towards your goals?

- What focus areas or ratios do you want to increase tomorrow?

Recommitment will take you farther than perfection. Kindness and self-compassion will take you farther than shame. If you're willing to keep referencing your compass, you're still on the path. You may not reach each destination exactly when you would like, but you will get there faster than intermittently abandoning the path out of doubt or frustration. Beyond that, life becomes much more of an adventure when we can embrace the step we are on today.

From Self-Criticism to Curiosity

Self-Criticism keeps us frozen. Curiosity sets us in motion. When you notice a behavior or choice you wish you had acted on differently, your first instinct might be to shame or scold yourself. But what if instead, you simply asked questions, such as:

"What was I feeling? What did I need? How would I prefer to approach this next time? Is there anything I need to address now, to resolve my current concerns? Is there any action I need to take, to make amends with someone else?"

You can let go of the idea that you're supposed to have it all figured out by now. Life isn't a pass/fail test, it's a practice. Curiosity keeps you engaged in that practice without quitting when it gets hard. Curiosity makes space. It helps shift your posture from needing control to consideration and care.

Seeking Purpose

Your purpose in life isn't always loud or obvious. It can begin as a whisper, a moment of captivation, a tug toward something that feels just a little bit more attuned to you. Sometimes, it's one clear direction. Other times, it's a constellation of interests and callings that change shape over time.

You don't need to declare a lifelong mission to live purposefully. You just need to say yes to what lights you up today. Those small yeses compound. They draw a path beneath your feet. It's a wonderful thing to pursue meaningful goals, yet it's equally important to stay present and seek purpose in the moment you are experiencing now. Sometimes, purpose reveals itself not through planning, but through how fully we show up right where we are.

It's worthwhile to make pursuing a purpose a part of your practice. This can mean checking in on your goals and how they might align to a meaningful path. This could include watching for connections between what you are finding excitement in pursuing now, and how it can support where you see yourself down the line.

While your main purpose doesn't have to be connected to your income, it doesn't hurt to consider it. If something feels useful and energizing to you, why not explore whether it could become part of your livelihood? Even if it doesn't generate profits immediately, or ever, it's worth evaluating the possibilities around what brings you happiness. If you look for ideas where your professional path can become more fulfilling over time, there's a higher chance you may find a way to align it with something that genuinely lights you up. An open mind combined with creativity can collectively open doors that were not there before.

At the same time, purpose is also found through practice. If nothing is sticking out today as a calling, perhaps you can instead focus on choosing to find meaning in your daily moments as your first step. By listening to your current desires and holding space for continued growth, you can balance progress and a joyful interaction with the present moment. That kind of attentiveness builds trust that today matters, and that if something can be improved, you'll sense it and respond when the time is right. It also builds gratitude in what you have, and appreciation for the world you are living in right now. This naturally builds a more open mind, through altering your state of being. This presence can connect you to flow, and from here the creative parts of your mind engage and expand.

Reflection:

- What feels purposeful to me today?

- Am I paying attention to enjoying little moments: *a smile, a laugh, smelling a flower?*

- Is there a path in life that is calling to me?

- Can I take any steps towards that direction right now?

- What might I be able to create and experience?

- How could I be open to new possibilities and apply creativity?

Noticing and Following Resonance

Resonance feels like the warmth of a campfire on a chilly night, or the cooling breeze of the ocean on a hot summer day. Like a full breath-in and out. Like the best part of your favorite song. When you notice that feeling, when something clicks or draws your attention in a concentrated and engaging way, pay attention. Following this resonance doesn't mean every path you take will be easy. But it does mean it will be *yours*. And that is what makes the effort worthwhile.

There is an interesting thing that happens when you respond to resonance; it makes it easier to hear next time. When you build a habit of leaning into this feeling, you'll start to feel its presence more consistently in your daily life. It will have more of a presence in guiding you to subtle signals of joy, energy, and peace. It may end up leading you somewhere new, where something that never resonated with you before ends up shining brightly, drawing you in that direction. Like a gold nugget sitting along the side of a stream, you have to get close enough to notice the sparkle. Seeking out these types of experiences makes you more open to being able to spot them when they come up.

Aligning with Your Natural Gifts

Another way to flow with life is through paying attention to your natural gifts and utilizing those gifts in your work, projects, and hobbies. It's not always easy for us to give ourselves credit where it is due, but practicing honesty in this area helps you to connect to these aspects of ourselves over time. It is useful to identify gaps and choose to grow them, but you don't always have to force yourself into improvement from the mindset of what is lacking. Sometimes, finding what is working and nurturing that is also worthwhile. It can also mean attaining more leverage in a shorter-time. In this scenario, you are simply noticing where the current is already heading and figuring out how to make that work best for you.

Living a fulfilling life can be supported through using your strengths in service of something that is valuable to the world. That doesn't mean doing this in a depleting way, where you are sacrificing your happiness or working nonstop. It means discovering where your natural talents, skills and your interests overlap, and letting that intersection guide your efforts. You could feel called to create, to heal, to build, to lead, to nurture, or to challenge old systems towards growth. You could try to build areas in your career, but you don't have to monetize it. You don't have to make it your job to find time for worthwhile activities. You just have to let it matter. Create space for it in your life.

When your energy is directed toward activities that feel real and resonant to you, you naturally stop asking, *"What's the point?"* and start feeling the answer in your day-to-day experiences. You redirect from seeking meaning and value externally and begin to realize that you are creating meaning in all of your interactions with the world around you. This isn't just for your benefit. Through embracing the unique connection that only you can share with those around you, the whole world benefits.

Reflection:

- What comes naturally to you?

- What brings you joy?

- What did you find yourself doing as a child?

- What activities do you get lost in?

- What brings you a sense of internal accomplishment?

If you aren't finding many answers, that doesn't mean there's nothing joyful to you. It means it's time to experiment. Trying some new things can help you discover what lights you up, both within yourself and in the opportunities around you. These small experiments often reveal overlooked passions or hidden strengths that reconnect you with your sense of potential and exuberance.

Chapter Summary

Recreating your life is not about finally getting it right, it's about returning again and again to what matters most. It's about deepening your understanding of your own priorities. It's about tuning into your sense of purpose, opening your mind to the possibilities, and learning to dance around the challenges rather than resist them. It's important to know where we want to go, and it's also important to choose to find purpose in every moment. This means a practice of seeing the beauty in the world as it is, and in ourselves as we are today. This moment is the only one you can act in, and accepting that allows you to take fuller breaths and find more appreciation in your heart.

You don't need to have a perfect answer. You just need a working compass and the willingness to follow it with consistency. Through recommitment, curiosity, resonance, and your natural qualities, you create a path that is uniquely yours. Keep choosing, keep listening, and trust that with each step, you're not just building a life. You're becoming the trust version of you, the one who naturally leads that life.

Chapter 8: Tending Relationships

As you build a life that reflects your internal compass, the relationships around you become even more important. They can either help steady your course or disrupt your progress. Either way, they challenge you to grow even further. They are one of the most rewarding parts of life. Our relationships give us the chance to see and be seen, know and be known, love and be loved.

Who you attract into your life can depend on your strengths and weaknesses. Often, we are drawn to people who either support our weaknesses, or push our buttons in a way that challenges us to address them and grow. This happens whether we realize it or not. The evolutions that occur from a relationship can lead to growing closer together, or in some cases, growing apart. Both people have an opportunity to examine their patterns and invite the potential for personal and aligned adaptation. This chapter explores the dynamics of relationships and provides recommendations on how to create relationships rooted in responsibility, honesty, and compassion.

Relationships are a Mirror

Our closest relationships reflect our inner patterns. This doesn't mean the people in our lives act exactly like we do, but it does mean there's something for us to learn when an emotional button is being pushed in a relationship. Feeling triggered is a chance to heal. It shows that a current exists and your awareness is turning to it, which means it's an opportunity to do something about it. Each time our buttons are pressed, there's a window of opportunity to take action towards healing. When we don't, we're effectively waiting for the same button to be pressed later.

Next we will go through a few common examples of imbalanced pairings that challenge us to grow. These are relational patterns, not complete representations of every relationship. They may resonate to different degrees, depending on each persons' experiences. In some cases you might resonate with neither, in some with both. In other cases, it might be only slightly resonant, where in others it feels very relatable. How these tendencies might be activated depends on individual relationships, as well as the context within a specific relationship. This isn't meant to be a complete model, but give attention to some trends, and offer an invitation to think more about balance and the patterns in your relationships.

Empathy vs Narcissism

An empathetic, or others-focused, partner may overextend themselves to accommodate, soothe, or please a more narcissistic, or self-focused, partner. The narcissistic partner may struggle, or not even try, to recognize the other's needs. The imbalance leads to burnout, resentment, or some loss of identity in the empathetic person. To address these outcomes, they must recognize their needs as equally valid and practice boundary-setting. This could even mean walking away, but even if so, healing is needed in the form of self compassion and reprioritization, to attract more caring people in their life. The more narcissistic partner needs to cultivate self-awareness and consider the impacts of their behavior, both to their partner and also themselves. It hurts them too, given narcissistic tendencies decrease their capacity to give and receive love, which requires openness and connection.

Dominant vs Submissive

Power imbalances can emerge when one partner regularly leads or controls decisions, possibly even being dismissive of the other partner. This happens while the other consistently yields, avoids conflict, or suppresses their needs. Submissiveness can result from learned dynamics, fear, or low self-esteem. The dominant partner would benefit from practicing humility, active listening, respectfulness, and shared decision-making. The submissive partner may need to strengthen their voice, develop self-trust, and practice self-respect. Both should learn to recognize that equality and respect foster true connection, not compliance.

Care-Free vs Care-Full

Disconnection often happens when one person is overwhelmed, consumed by responsibilities, and their need for caution and care is excessively full. Meanwhile, the other seems disengaged, avoidant, or careless. The care-full individual may feel unsupported, stressed, and resentful, while the care-free partner may feel criticized, immature, or blame the care-full partner for being unhappy. To find balance, the care-full partner may need to release some control, ask for help more directly, and seek joyful experiences more often, while the care-free partner may need to take on more responsibilities, emphasize practicality, and develop their reliability.

Conflict Avoidant vs Reactionary

How we address conflicts and triggers can vary deeply. One partner might excessively avoid conflicts, walking on eggshells to keep things calm and minimize their own needs. The other might express unmet needs through emotional outbursts or volatility. The avoidant partner must learn to speak up and be able to face challenges for better outcomes, and the reactive partner must learn to regulate their emotions and communicate their needs in a way that respects the needs of their partner as well.

Fixer vs Self-Sabotaging

The fixer wants to heal, support, and uplift, but is still drawn to someone who isn't willing to do their own work for self-improvement. The self-sabotaging partner may be caught in a cycle of hopelessness, and may resist progress or even sabotage efforts to help them. The fixer may end up feeling exhausted and lonely. The helper must practice letting go of responsibility for others and honoring limits, while the self-sabotaging partner should investigate reasons for their current mindset, and begin taking acts of agency. This can help them believe in their ability to grow rather than taking a passive stance, depending on, and then resisting help from others.

Past-Focused vs Past-Avoidant

When you are living in the past, it's often because you are afraid of making the same mistakes or having someone in your life make the same choices and hurt you again. When you stay in this space excessively, it burns up a lot of your energy and robs you of your ability to experience and utilize the present moment to the fullest. When you are living in the present moment in a way that you are being avoidant of the past, usually those emotions are just below the surface...waiting, unresolved. Being unwilling to face the past also typically means you lack the wisdom you needed to gain from doing an honest analysis of what happened and what you could learn from it. Life is a dance of balancing. When you embrace this, you can seek reflection to obtain the wisdom necessary, and then let go. This allows you to relax into the present moment and thoughtfully apply what you've learned to what you choose now and move forward.

Reflection:

- What patterns do I see repeating in my close relationships?

- What are they showing me about current boundaries?

- Do I see relationships in my life that could be more balanced?

- What related beliefs do I have that could be improved?

- What do I want to change personally?

- What do I need to ask for from others?

Relationships Require Care

When you bring different people together, it's inevitable there will be conflict. After all, a conflict is just a difference being expressed. There doesn't have to be such a negative connotation to conflicts. They may bring some discomfort, but they also offer many benefits. They can bring opportunities for change and growth, understanding, and expression of care through partnership in facing challenges together. It takes effort to work through having different perspectives, but it's also an invitation to broaden your perspective by visiting someone else's view for a while. It doesn't mean you have to change your mind entirely and mimic how things appear in their mind, it just means you can see further along the horizon of experiences.

When conflicts arise, consider whose need is more intense at that moment. If you think about how important a particular issue is to you, and how important it is to the other person, you might look at the approach forward differently. Be happy to give, not every time, but when you truly believe the other person needs more support. Practice feeling content in giving them what they need in the moment, which lifts you up too. Be happy to receive as well. Some people find accepting support challenging. If you feel guilty receiving from others, remember giving is a healthy part of a relationship and should go both ways. If you struggle with this, take a moment to appreciate the sacrifice they made. Notice how it can nurture you, feel this sinking in, and let them know it matters to you. Watch for how it uplifts them to give to you.

A lot of conflict comes from our prior experiences, we tend to project our fears on others based on the pain of our past. It's natural to want to watch out for things that have hurt you, so you can protect yourself from the same pain again. However, as we've discussed already, what you focus on impacts your reality. If your focus towards the past hurts is left unchecked, difficult experiences can result in creating an environment allowing repetition. Through focusing on the fear, some people even imagine the same thing is happening in a case where it actively is not. They create it in their experience, despite it being resolved in their current circumstances. Actively noticing when you're focusing on past pain allows you to take charge of your mind instead. Then you are empowered to switch your focus to what you want to create. If you notice others are doing this, understanding the mechanisms can increase your capacity to compassionately approach the issue with them and help them see an opportunity to address it.

Honest communication alongside repair also requires a lot of effort. Expressing your truth doesn't just mean focusing on yourself, it means communicating without expecting to control the outcome. It means still monitoring yourself to ensure you aren't involuntarily or purposefully attacking the other person. This takes practice, because it means you're also monitoring what you allow to become true in your mind. This can be hard, especially at times where intense emotions are involved. It can be challenging to communicate openly without feeling the need to agree. Putting forth the effort to be honest, even without knowing how the other person will respond, and being courageous enough to sit with that discomfort. It is also a challenge as the listening party. It can be complex to acknowledge the other person's experience without falsely agreeing, knowing any conflicts may make both of you uncomfortable, and expressing your differences in opinion anyways.

The most important thing to prevail through any sort of turmoil is navigating misalignment and repairing with compassion for each other. If you add in the intent to understand, even if you don't agree, it opens space for other emotions. Seeing the others' side and practicing holding this space: intending wellness and love for them, even while you are feeling uncomfortable, really changes the tone of any disagreement. Rather than being opposed to each other, you are simply experiencing a disagreement that can likely be resolved. Solutions could be identified with many different approaches: accommodation, compromise, acceptance, creative problem solving, negotiation, etc.

Even in the cases where people truly want completely different things and it's unresolvable in terms of maintaining the relationship, there can still be understanding, care, and grace towards each other. If this was really the case, would you rather live a lie, or let go lovingly? The benefit to living from a place of truth, compassion, and responsibility ultimately supports you and those you interact with in ways you may not be able to see today.

Reflection:

- How do I respond to conflict or unmet needs currently?

- What can I improve about my communication style and habits?

- Do I invite openness in others?

- Do I communicate as honestly as I would like?

- What types of relationships do I want in my life right now?

- What do I want to build in these relationships?

Healthy vs Harmful Bonds

Relationships require give and take. If that balance is off, it may be time to consciously add weight to the scale. There is a chance the relationship could change to adapt to this version of you, that has better boundaries. However, sometimes these changes cause clarity that the relationship is not working and won't adapt in the necessary ways, and it's time to let someone go who isn't fitting into your life anymore. When you leave plants in the garden, whether you planted them or not, they still take resources away from other plants. In relationships, this is true as well.

But sometimes people keep expired relationships in their lives for the wrong reasons. Not because they truly value and want the relationship, including the work to improve it, but instead because of codependency, fear of the unknown, or guilt-based loyalty. If the relationship is continuing only because you aren't addressing something in your life, then that gap should be evaluated. Is it something you can and are willing to address?

It's also important to understand what the interaction is at its core: connection with true depth or emotional ties? Maintaining emotional ties out of habit can result in managing not only your own emotions, but also the emotional experiences of those around you. This might look like soothing, adjusting your behavior to avoid triggering others, or taking responsibility for maintaining harmony. While caring for others is beautiful, when it becomes an expectation or obligation without mutual emotional reciprocity, it becomes draining. Emotional connection, by contrast, is mutually nourishing. It's based on openness, co-regulation, and shared emotional presence.

In balanced relationships, both people feel seen, supported, and emotionally safe, not because one person is over-functioning, but because both are showing up. At times one person may need to take on more to help the other while they are going through a higher emotional burden. However, the work should be balanced when you look at the relationship over time. This doesn't mean the relationship is perfect or without issue, but it feels real and meaningful.

Relationships are supposed to involve work. The question is: *is this relationship worth the effort it's costing?* When you're frustrated, be aware of the benefits and genuinely evaluate whether it's a net positive in your life. Is it just a rough time; maybe the ebb and flow of the other person's needs is just a bit more turbulent right now, or is the synchronicity really not there? Relationships can include a lot of win-win solutions. However, not all situations offer a win-win outcome. Sometimes we give, sometimes we take, but the overarching outcomes should generally provide more value, joy, and love to both people with all things considered.

Another important factor is whether trust currently exists, and if not, whether it can realistically be rebuilt. A lot of people question the ability to rebuild trust after disappointment. It is possible, but it's more complex than just saying you will. Often this issue is spoken of with an overly simplified definition, saying that either the hurt party needs to *let go of the past*, or the offending party needs to *make amends*. But both have to happen. The person who had their trust broken has to want to forgive, but more importantly, the person who broke the trust has to attain the wisdom to address what was involved in their choice of the untrustworthy action in the first place.

If they were afraid, why? How will they have more courage and strength next time? If they were angry, why? How would they handle it differently in the future? If the expectation is put on one person in the relationship to repair trust, there can be gaps remaining. If it's only on the trust breaker but lacking clear expectations, they might not be able to figure out how to action the solution alone. If the person who lost trust is expected to get over it without clear change indicating the same thing won't be repeated, it's much less likely to work. If you can relate to either perspective, it's worth asking:

For the forgiver:

- *Do I want to forgive, if I see clear and real change?*

- *What do I need, specifically?*

For the forgiven:

- *Do I want to do the work to repair the trust I broke?*

- *How exactly will I do that?*

Reflection:

- Are there relationships in my life where I feel drained?

- Do I feel these relationships are balanced over time?

- Do any require healthier boundaries or renegotiation?

- How can I make more space to nourish others in my life?

- What relationships do I value most in my life?

- How do I give and receive in my relationships?

- What would relationships with more resonance look like?

Selecting Your Relationships

It's important to evaluate who you want in your life, over continued accommodation of the same people, just because they have been in your proximity historically. This evaluation can apply to any type of relationship. This is especially important in romantic partnerships, since these individuals get the most of your time and have the highest impact on you. They receive more of your energy compared to anyone else, and this can greatly support or deplete you, depending on the health of the relationship and its alignment to what you want out of your life.

One of the first steps to improving your relationships is taking more responsibility for your own actions. It's very easy to notice when our own needs aren't being met, but it can be a bit more difficult to notice where we might be falling short. It helps to ask ourselves:

Am I taking responsibility to act in accordance with my principles and expectations? Am I clearly defining and communicating those expectations and holding the boundaries with others?

If you want to find and build relationships that reflect your values, the first step is to live by them yourself. That internal alignment shapes who you attract, how you show up, and how you ask for the same in return. Living by your truth creates space to receive likeness. While everyone has to identify what they are willing to live by, and what they expect, here are some common examples of priority values:

Honesty

A lot of people oversimplify what being honest really means. It's not just avoiding constant lying, or lying about "big" things. Being genuinely honest means being ready with strength to bear speaking uncomfortable truths, no matter the size. Facing these types of issues directly requires deeper vulnerability, but empowers both parties in the relationship to be heard and take action to address issues. Sometimes the result is practicing acceptance, identifying solutions, or addressing the need for new approaches. It also allows those being honest to relax into themselves, and feel more present and at ease in life.

Integrity

Acting in alignment with your chosen values strengthens your credibility and creates stability when interacting with others. It reduces confusion, invites accountability, and models consistency through dedication. Integrity helps others feel safe, given they understand what they can expect from you.

Respect

Honoring each other's boundaries, time, and unique traits fosters trust and understanding. Respect means listening with the intent to really take in their perspective, not just to reply. It allows both people to feel seen and valued as whole human beings, rather than only through the lens of the role they play in each other's lives.

Presence

Being emotionally and mentally available when you're together builds depth and appreciation in any relationship. It's not just about physical proximity, it's about awareness and attention. Practicing presence can help improve connections, because people feel valued when they're truly noticed. It is also foundational to intimacy and joy.

Growth

Supporting each other's evolution is important, rather than expecting certainty through staying the same over time. When we expect static identity, we can accidentally stunt each other, or lose connection with our true selves by trying to stay who we used to be. Growth invites curiosity, flexibility, and celebration of changes. In relationships it also means encouraging each other's growth, and when that challenges us, seeking ways to improve ourselves too. Sometimes people do grow apart, but when you're welcoming growth in each other, that gives the relationship much more room to adapt and figure out new dynamics that support ongoing adaptations.

Reciprocity

Balanced relationships include give and take that is responsive, not calculated. When both people feel supported, safe, and empowered to contribute, the relationship builds momentum in their lives rather than draining it. Addressing one-sidedness with honesty can create room to restore harmony, depending on how those involved respond. One-sidedness can be complex and is very much based on perception; people give differently. For example, one may give more in emotional support while the other gives more in financial support. The main questions are whether all effort is appreciated, and if both parties are receiving in ways that meet their needs.

Reliability

Being dependable, both in a physical and emotional sense, creates the scaffolding for trust. It helps soothe fear, lower defensiveness, and build a steady foundation for vulnerability. Both people should be able to count on each other, as they carefully make and stick to their commitments.

Playfulness

Sharing adventure, humor, or silliness can help regulate stress and build emotional connection. Playfulness keeps relationships resilient, as it reminds us that joy is a form of bonding. Fun doesn't have to disappear as relationships deepen. The novelty of a new relationship can be exciting, but it can be even more exciting to make a long-term committed relationship more novel by intentionally turning life into a playful journey ventured together.

Gratitude

Expressing appreciation aloud in your relationships cultivates warmth and love. It also encourages more of the behavior that makes you feel cared for. Gratitude makes it easier to navigate the hard parts of relationships, because it reinforces connection and peace. It also enhances the best parts of relationships, because you are making the space to really take these moments in.

Commitment

Conflict happens in all relationships. The big question determining whether the relationship can weather these conflicts is: *Do the people involved choose to reconnect afterwards?* Relationships thrive when repair is practiced intentionally and regardless of ease. This includes apologies, reflection, and changed behavior, not just saying sorry. When individuals are committed, a way through most challenges can be found.

Loyalty

The level of loyalty people need to feel differs across relationships. It starts with understanding and agreeing on what boundaries should look like in detail. Agreeing on them is only one step. It's just as important to set up boundaries that you are also willing to abide by. Choosing them and maintaining them builds shared expectations and reinforces a foundation of mutual respect and trust.

Chapter Summary

People usually think of love as something that draws us to one another. As if love is the ingredient that makes us want someone in our lives. But I would argue love isn't the wanting, it's the energy we get to experience when we choose to maintain someone as a part of our lives. And who we choose, and why we choose them, impacts the amount of love that can be present in the relationship. Wanting someone has to do with a complex combination of aspects of ourselves: our ego, goals, desires, boundaries, etc., and their traits as well. But it's important to remember that choosing people to care about and give our focus, simply makes space to experience love. The more effort we put in with humility and care, the more we will get out of it. It's a beautiful thing to get to experience with anyone, and can be fostered simply with the intention.

Tending to your relationships is like tending to a garden. Each one requires attention, pruning, nurturing, and sometimes, even replanting. As your inner life evolves, your outer relationships deserve the same level of intention setting as well. The more care you bring to your relationships, through honesty, effort, commitments, and gratitude, the more space you create for growth, safety, support, and joy on your journey.

Part III:

Finding Your True Path

Chapter 9: Connecting to Nature

We are not separate from nature, we are part of it. Yet so much of the modern current pulls us into artificial rhythms: productivity over presence, perfection over iteration, isolation over incorporation, wealth over wellness. In this chapter we explore how reconnecting with the natural world can gently return us to this moment, increase our experiences of wellbeing, and connect to our deepest inner truths.

It's funny that I chose a river as the challenging factor in this analogy. I probably was drawn to this imagery to explain, and help other people incorporate lessons I've learned, because to me a river feels like the most safe and centering place I can think of. I spent a lot of time during my childhood swimming in the river, and it always felt very healing, strengthening, and welcoming to me.

I hope I've made it clear so far, these currents are simply to be noticed and worked with. Once we see how they're flowing around us and pushing us, we get to decide whether we like it as it is, or want to make changes. If we want to change, we do our part to get ourselves into currents that are more suitable to us. We wouldn't want to spend all day swimming in waters that were too fast, rocky, or turbulent. With that said, it doesn't have to be a critical judgement if you notice that's where you are right now. We don't choose where we start, but we do choose where we go. That of course assumes we're willing to do the work. Nature can help strengthen us and nurture us on our journey to finding our favorite waters.

Why Nature Matters

We come from nature. We are biological creatures that are meant to be connected to the natural world. This doesn't mean we have to spend 100% of our time in the great outdoors, but it is important that we don't forget this key attribute about who we are. Nature tells us stories about natural law through the ways it shapes and transforms itself. When our ancestors spent all of their time in nature, they were directly connected to these fundamental truths in ways we often forget or minimize in modern society. For instance, everything we do, large and small, has a cost and a benefit. They had reminders of this every day; foraging, hunting, traveling, all cost time, stamina, and require physical refueling (e.g. calories). While we may be aware of a relationship's cost and benefit logically, we have lost sight of an intuitive and ever present relationship with this attribute of our existence.

With all of the conveniences and distractions of our environment today, it is easy to forget, everything does have a cost and benefit that shapes what is profound and meaningful. Even what we eat has a life, an experience, growing for months or years. A few hours of scrolling online seems so small and can provide entertainment to you, but it also costs your time. We trick ourselves into feeling like time is unlimited, but even today we still only have so much of it. Using time also costs potential value share with the world or income earned for us. With that said, we can also utilize the resources provided by online content to improve ourselves, our relationships, and overall lifestyle. The important thing isn't drastic change, that we more fully understand and accept the costs of what we choose.

Many people find that time in nature helps them feel more peaceful, calm, and emotionally balanced. The pace of the natural world invites us to slow down, breathe deeply, and feel grounded. Cycles in nature mirror our own internal rhythms: growth, play, letting go, and rest. All of these seasons have a role in our own renewal and vitality. Tuning into nature can help create more balance within ourselves, simply by listening. Disconnection from nature often mirrors disconnection from our own bodies and intuition, so spending time in nature may be one of the most powerful ways to reconnect and restore harmony in body, mind, and spirit.

Ways to Reconnect

I bet you've already heard the term: *can't see the forest for the trees*. Have you ever reflected on the meaning of this? Have you ever sat within trees and sought to witness the forest? Intentionally set your focus and mind towards taking in the forest? Noticing the small details of the plants, animals, and insects? If not, it could be worth a try. You may find more than you would imagine. There's often meaning beyond the logical intent, when we invite curiosity to discover with our full mind engaged. If you have tried something like this, it can't hurt to practice again. The more time we spend simplifying, listening, and connecting, the more the wonder of nature calls to us and restores our sense of peace and healing.

If sitting quietly in a mindful or meditative state seems unrelatable to you right now, you could find something else that works for you. For instance, walking outside without headphones and allowing the sensory input to ground you. Or even walking outside while listening to an audiobook, podcast, or music, could invite connection to nature that fits your lifestyle. If you are listening to music, just be sure you are in a safe space and aware of your surroundings.

If you're willing to dig a bit deeper, tending to a plant or garden can be an exceptional way to reconnect with nature. By choosing this activity, you are engaging with slow growth and practicing patience, nurturing, and consistency of your presence. If you grow a garden, it's also a practice of connecting with and feeling gratitude for your food. If you want to go even a step further like me, you can plant some perennial plants or even a food forest. With this approach, you get to watch them grow over time and look forward to the harvest they bring to you, year after year. Any form of gardening can also foster a sense of self-sufficiency, and may help reduce grocery costs over time which is another fun benefit.

Your time in nature doesn't have to be a major life change though. One day at a time, you can choose moments to reflect and appreciate nature such as:

- Watching a sunrise or sunset to recalibrate your sense of time.

- Going outside and noticing if your emotions change.

- Getting close to a tree and noticing how complex it is.

- Going to a park to appreciate plants, remember they are inhaling your carbon dioxide, as you inhale their oxygen.

- Take moments to notice the seasons and what they evoke.

Visualizations For Connecting With Nature

Guided meditations can be a wonderful tool for recalibrating and training our minds to function more in alignment to what we prefer. Combining this with nature can have remarkable benefits. This doesn't have to be complex. Even simply sitting outside with the intention of letting thoughts smoothly come and go could change your day. Whether you are quieting the mind and witnessing the environment, or trying exercises with visualizations, you are utilizing nature as a teacher. In this section, you will have some options to try that enhance feelings of a deeper connection to the natural world. This can help ground, nurture, and strengthen you.

River Meditation: Flow and Acceptance

Close your eyes and imagine yourself floating in a wide and calm river. The water carries you gently. You don't resist, you trust the current is where it needs to be today, and life is leading you somewhere meaningful. You know that you will move and change your direction later, but right now, you are allowing yourself to rest into the current flow. Let your thoughts drift by like leaves on the surface. Breathe deeply and let the movement ease your tension. Feel the waters cleansing you, and bringing you what you need.

Tree Meditation: Rootedness and Flexibility

Sit comfortably, preferably outside or by a window. Imagine yourself as a tree. Feel your spine grow tall like a trunk, and your feet or hips settle into the earth like roots spreading outward. Imagine these roots drawing up nourishment, support, and stability. As the winds of life blow through your branches, you sway, but you do not break. You are grounded and adaptable.

You are firm yet flexible. As you grow you reach upward, grateful to the sun and sky, always learning and creating new expressions of yourself.

Mountain Meditation: Perspective and Stillness

Visualize yourself on a quiet mountaintop. You are high above the noise, witnessing what is below with clarity and perspective. The wind blows, but you are steady and stable. Inside you is stillness and strength. Each breath expands your awareness and connection to everything below. Notice how small daily stressors appear from this vantage point. Feel the density of the stone surface beneath you, a reminder that peace can be both powerful and safe.

Sky Meditation: Impermanence and Presence

Picture the sky above you. Notice how it is vast, open, and ever-changing. Clouds drift in and out of view, some heavy, some light. Some bring rain and thunder, while others make way for the sun. Even the rain clouds bring replenishment and purification. These clouds represent your thoughts, emotions, and experiences. You are the sky, not the clouds. Let each pass without judgment. Notice the space they come and go within. Appreciate this space and the room it makes for starry nights and beautiful sunsets.

Reflection:

- When do I feel most connected to the natural world?

- What happens in my body and mind as I spend time outdoors?

- What lessons from nature resonate with me?

- What current challenges could nature help me navigate?

- What are my favorite things to do in nature?

Chapter Summary

The natural world is not just scenery, it is a *mentor and healer*. It provides us a subtle invitation to return to presence, balance, and relational wholeness. It is our foundation, where we come from, and our home. The more we return to nature, the more we naturally accept from a deep wellspring of nurturing and connection. As we return to nature we can also find new ways to appreciate, respect, and care for it across our choices and innovations.

Chapter 10: The Purpose Beyond Self

There comes a time when the need for healing softens and more of your energy can begin to shift from inward restoration to outward expansion. Much like water smoothing stone over time, the intense tides of your emotions begin to settle, allowing space for deeper connection and contribution to emerge. This doesn't mean you're "done" with growth. You've simply grown roots that are established enough to stabilize you and support your outward reach. This allows your branches to reach farther, as you are ascending upwards and expanding your presence in the world. As you align in body, mind, and soul, you can begin to connect with something bigger than yourself. You begin to feel the drawing, to offer something of yourself and from yourself to those around you.

When it's a true calling, you decide to contribute not because you would feel bad if you don't. It is because you're ready and genuinely feel inspired to. This brings about experiencing purpose beyond self. The gift that flows not from depletion, but from wholeness. That benefits not just others, but also you, down to your core.

From Stabilization to Service

Contribution becomes most sustainable after your own *regulation and healing*. You don't have to wait until you're at 100% of your potential to be able to contribute, but the more you build yourself up, balance, and reach wellness, the more you can give without depleting yourself. To give from a place of lack can feel momentarily uplifting, offering a short-term emotional boost. But without replenishment for inner balance, such giving often becomes unsustainable. This can drain your energy over time and risk causing burnout. Consider whether your giving uplifts both yourself and others, and whether it supports your long-term balance and vitality. If you force yourself to give more than you have to offer, it can eventually become detrimental to your growth. It's not about giving the most, it's about giving in a way you can support over time. After all, giving a little today, tomorrow, and the next day, will often result in a larger offering than if you were to only go all out today. In addition, you'll probably have a better time not rushing yourself, and feeling more contentment and peace in the process.

The goal for yourself shouldn't be perfection, it's more about being resourced enough to enjoy your life and share in that joy. Purpose expands when you stop asking only *"what do I need?"* and start also asking *"what do I want to offer?"* This perspective can be one of the best fuels for your own growth. As you trust yourself more and more, moving towards doing good in the world can push you even further. Not in a "burn out" kind of way, but into a meaning driven reality. The part of us that tends to criticize ourselves can't talk us out of a goal so easily when we know deep down the outcomes of our self-improvements, effort, and healing won't end with us.

Why It Matters to Give

Let's begin with this idea: meaning involves participation and engagement with the world around us. We are designed to be social creatures. What helped humans survive in nature and thrive even when facing the wildest of predators wasn't just our brains, it was also our community. We've evolved to support, tend to, nurture, and have fun together, and what a gift this is. It can be forgotten with all of the distractions of today's world, but it can just as easily be remembered.

Giving pulls us out of stagnation, isolation, and over-identification with the self. It creates a feedback loop of vitality and hope, rather than a feedback loop of lack, fear, and criticism. It helps us to refocus on becoming our own source and example of creativity in the world, rather than focusing on the judgement and destruction that exists externally. As more of us become beacons of positivity and hope, it can change the larger ecosystem fundamentally. It only takes one person at a time to create a compounding shift.

When you tend to something greater than yourself, you are also reminded that you are not alone. For example, if you design and tend to a garden, it can remind you how nature coexists, cooperates, and supports the surrounding ecosystem as well as itself. You see the bees pollinate the flowers as they gather honey. You witness the sun glowing on the leaves as they photosynthesize. You see mushrooms breaking down plant matter and supporting the entire system with nutrients. Eventually you see fruits become ripe from these collective efforts. The fruits of your work, paired with the work of the ecosystem, eventually produce berries that you get to eat right off the bush. This can naturally make you start to wonder: "What will I grow that I can share?"

Contribution ≠ Sacrifice

Now let's investigate the boundaries that would need to exist to sustain this garden. Imagine that you did create a beautiful and bountiful garden you now want to share from. If you were living on the harvest from this garden, you could certainly share once you had developed skills in gardening, and had a surplus due to your level of experience and collective time spent. And you can obviously see how if you were to give away everything in your garden, or most of what was coming from your garden, you could starve. You wouldn't have enough for yourself, and thus also wouldn't have the energy to sustain the garden. Not sacrificing yourself isn't a "nice to have" when bringing positivity in the world long-term, it's a necessity.

In some cases heroes do choose to sacrifice themselves, but there is a cost. Those types of sacrifices are meaningful, but it doesn't have to be your story in order to be of service. If you want to create lasting impact over time, the way to do so is through taking care of yourself in the process. You might be able to temporarily be overgenerous and tell yourself it's fine, just because so far you haven't completely burnt out. But giving away too much will compound over time. In the short-term you can do this, but you need to replenish yourself to return to "wellness". If you listen you can feel the truth. If you honestly ask if you're putting yourself into a deficit, you will know. Creating sustainable change is possible, and asking will tell you what you need to know to find a path towards this balance. Sustainability in contribution is not selfish, it's sacred. It's treating yourself with the same love you intend to share with everyone else.

Listening for What's Yours

Things can feel very lonely in the modern age. We've evolved so quickly, but our bias towards noticing danger is as strong as ever. When you pair that with access to global and instantaneous information sharing, it can become overwhelming. One of the most beautiful things about us is our ability to empathize. However, this too can begin to feel like a detriment rather than a gift. It is possible to return empathy to a positive means of finding space for action. When you can do something positive with empathy, as it is intended, it feels completely different than diffused attention and grief spread across the world.

When you make a positive change in someone else's day, instead of being drained you are fueled by that same capacity for empathy. This experience can help us remember how wonderful empathy can be, and let go of the need to carry every negative feeling we encounter. We are only one person, living one life, and only able to impact some of the lives of people we will hear about. Realigning to this realism and not shutting down empathy, but focusing it can help us reserve the energy needed to make real change, in the areas we care about most.

To build on that idea: purpose should not burn you out, it should *energize and engage you*. If it feels like it is burning you out, it may be time to question the *why* behind holding onto that purpose. True purpose can drive you without relying on the fuel of fear, worry, anger, guilt or shame. It shouldn't be expected to be boundless action, but intentional and directed towards something that resonates with you. Explore what *purposeful contribution* looks like to you, not necessarily massive in scope, but instead *meaningful*. It could be caregiving, creativity, advocacy, work, mentoring, parenting, volunteering, or building new innovations and systems.

Not every cause is yours to carry. Not every thought requires further attention. Not every idea needs to be yours for action. It is such an easy mindset trap to fall into in today's era, that we have to be passionate about and involved in everything. But again, if you take a moment to really reflect on this, it becomes so clear this isn't actually achievable. Being passionate is an important part of life, but there's an energy cost. If you yell about something that has deeply hurt you or someone you care about for an hour, sure that could be healthy venting, but imagine if you do it for an entire day. You aren't going to have much energy to take action afterwards. This doesn't mean there isn't a time and place. But it's important to understand the cost of exerting intensity and being intentional about how, why, and when we do this. If we engage passionately about every political topic that comes up, where is that energy going, and is it worth it? Are all of these issues actually that personal to us? Did the dispersion across so many areas leave adequate reserves to deeply engage on the one or two that are profoundly important to us?

When you notice what is obligation vs true resonance, you can get so much of your power and energy back. It's completely fair to say "this is not my fight" sometimes, and possible to do so while still being compassionate to others. It shouldn't become an excuse to be disengaged from the world around you. It's about having compassion globally but empathizing locally. This saves the reserves to be intentional with your focus. Unless you intend to do something about it, focus can be limited to trying to understand others a little better. When you are going to do something about it, having more of your focus freed up gives you waves of potential to make real change. This doesn't have to be all at once, trust that small contributions matter. You don't always need a platform or the loudest megaphone, just integrity as your compass and consistency in your commitments.

Sustainable Contribution Through Business

This section doesn't have to apply to everyone. If you want to skip it, that's okay. For many it won't apply today but might plant a seed of inspiration that grows when the timing is right. It doesn't need to be pressure, just an idea that you can play with. It might not resonate for you or it might resonate without a clear picture. As it begins to resonate, you begin to make space for the vision to grow. What might feel impossible now may eventually feel obvious or necessary in a month, or a year, or 10 years down the line. If you make space for these ideas to grow, you may be surprised what can become of them.

Building a business that you enjoy, and that allows you to express your values, creativity, and unique experience, is one of the most aligned and powerful ways to live your purpose. When your work energizes you instead of draining you, and when it helps others in the process, you're creating a regenerative cycle. Your effort builds you, and it builds something worthwhile for others too. The concept doesn't need to be the fastest, largest, or best, it just needs to bring value into the world.

This doesn't mean every day is easy or every challenge is enjoyable, but it does mean that the challenges are worth navigating because they serve a bigger *why*. Your business becomes not just a job or a product, but a vessel for expression with reason behind it. Done intentionally, this kind of contribution can scale in both impact and sustainability, helping you show up fully and engage passionately without depleting yourself. If you build it around the values that matter most to you, your business becomes a form of activism, healing, and hope all in one.

Reflection:

- Where do I feel called to contribute at this time?

- What part of me feels most alive when I'm giving?

- What issues have I been paying attention to that feel draining?

- Where am I trying to help from guilt or excessive-responsibility?

- What roles or causes feel aligned and energizing to me?

- What are my strengths and how can they support others?

- How would the deepest intentional contribution look?

Chapter Summary

Helping others isn't always about being a hero, it's often about being a participant. It's about showing up, consistently and authentically, because your unique presence and contribution matter. Purpose doesn't require a grand gesture or a perfect plan. It simply asks that you begin where you are, with what you have, and engage from a place of care. It asks only that you notice what moves you and follow the small impulses to take action, to create, and to connect.

Let your sense of purpose be shaped not by pressure, but by resonance. Let it grow from within you, not because you feel lacking without it, but instead because you want to welcome the light of caring into your heart.

Contribution is not a destination. It is best when it comes not out of obligation, but out of love. When you choose not to singlehandedly save the world, but to act in it with honesty, courage, and strength. Because in that participation, you will find a new kind of fulfillment. What if the big thing you've been waiting to find has been quietly waiting for you to notice that it is this simple all along?

Chapter 11: Turning the Tides

Changing Together

Imagine a culture where flaunting your yacht is not impressive without some acknowledgement of philanthropy. Where this kind of celebration of wealth also comes with an expectation from your peers to share how you're contributing to the world. This could be in your own unique expression of caring; anything that somehow improves the wellbeing of other people, animals, the environment, etc. In this reality wealth signals responsibility, not simply the potential for overindulgence. Where hoarding resources while others suffer is not just frowned upon, but considered embarrassing.

A culture where freedom is honored, but always paired with the expectation of a self-imposed responsibility to act according to principles that are conscious of the greater good. Where our choices reflect a deeper care for the world around us, for one another, and for future generations. Not out of force or perceived superiority, but where reasonable and consistent social pressure gently encourages each other to consider how we give and receive kindness, and to practice both with greater depth and sincerity.

To keep improving as a species, we need social gravity that pulls us towards collective good over individual excess. It's important that this culture also does not shame us for wanting to grow and celebrate our wins. That moves us toward balance instead of burnout. Enables satisfaction and connection, instead of a lie that your worth depends on having more. Leaning too far to either extreme means either punishing yourself and discouraging effort, or glorifying empty pleasure.

If we lived in a culture that integrates the positives of reaching and achieving, with compassion and duty, we would strive individually to build a better future together. For example, this could include both aspects of holistic and natural living, integrated with thoughtful and careful innovation. One that values morality, virtue, and sustainability as markers of true success. And as individuals, we can shift towards this reality one mind at a time. It begins with choosing what we support wisely, through how we live, what we consume, and what we stand for.

When I was a little girl, my grandparents had a small above-ground pool. A standard one, that stood a few feet tall and was circular in shape. I always loved being in the water. When I was visiting them, I wanted to be in that pool as often as possible. Sometimes my grandmother would start a game where everyone in the pool would walk the same direction. At different speeds, at their own pace, but still cycling together. I loved this game, feeling the current form from our collective efforts. I was the smallest in the pool at many of these gatherings, so when enough people were involved, I'd get swept up in the current. I found it thrilling. I'd pick up my feet and let the water carry me, giggling. Sometimes I'd try to get the current going myself when the adults and older children had enough of the pool. I could manage a bit of movement, but it always picked up faster and stronger when I had others join me in the water.

Cultural change works like this too. We can at times move on our own, and this momentum matters. It's harder to be at the forefront of change but it's also deeply meaningful. That extra work makes us stronger, and often, it inspires others to join us. This means the eventual amplification of the impact of our efforts. With every step we take, the current strengthens with us.

Change is Inevitable

Change can feel scary. Whether we notice it or not, a lot of us spend a significant amount of our time avoiding change. This is to differing degrees, between different people and the phases of our lives. Even for those of us who put forth active effort to welcome and seek positive changes, there is still some animal instinct in our minds pushing against change in an attempt to keep us safe from unknown risks and harm. This makes sense, from a survival standpoint. For instance, if you can't tell where you're going at night you might run into a predator. Or if you are running too fast you might fall off a cliff. But that doesn't mean we should stop moving forward, instead proceed with care and diligence. Create our own torch, and thoughtfully press forward.

At other times, it can feel like things don't actually change. We see patterns repeating in our lives that we don't like and feel discouraged. But even in our loneliest, most stagnant moments, life is still moving. The current doesn't disappear; it sometimes flows quietly beneath our awareness. Like a river shrouded in fog, or a heartbeat unnoticed until the silence, it waits for the return of our focus. When we feel disconnected it is often our attention, not our access, that has shifted. When we shift our focus back to what better supports us, things go even further towards what we do want. Things start to shift when we combine putting forth effort to create desired changes with making space for them. Things start to move again, not always immediately, but change does happen day by day, and this compounds over time.

Time being necessary for change is actually good for us. If things changed imminently, as soon as we had a thought, that could be a negative experience in many ways. If as soon as we worried we might fall, we fell. If as soon as we feared we would be rude, we said something with no grace. If as soon as we thought we might be bad at something, we were. Our minds tend to accidentally seek negative experiences as a result of being hard wired to look for danger. The time it takes for thoughts to compound gives us the space to be intentional in what thoughts we feed, and which we let go. Which we intentionally reproduce to build more of that narrative in our minds, and to draw more of those desired circumstances in our realities.

Because change is inevitable, it only makes sense that we put forth effort as part of our existence to create the types of changes we want to see. Rather than waiting for something to happen, we might as well embrace and be selective about inviting change.

Changing Ourselves

We are living in a time of immense pressure and pace. Despite unprecedented access to technology and convenience, many people are lonelier, more anxious, more disconnected from nature and community than ever before. We chase more, faster, and better; often at the cost of our relationships, our peace, and our health. Burnout is exceedingly more common. Disillusionment is spreading. Division is extreme. Many are searching for purpose in a culture that prizes ego over authenticity. Authenticity is even thrown around as a buzz word, with many people forgetting what it means to be genuinely true to yourself. That it doesn't put you on a pedestal, it means doing the challenging work to become better, and stand up to conflict, but also discern when that is truly necessary. Not to be selfish, simply to be real.

We live so much of our lives elsewhere: in yesterday's replays, tomorrow's worries, and fear based scenarios that never occur. But the current of our life always flows through the present moment. If we want to change the course we're heading down, we have to learn to be here now. To feel our own breath. To notice the ground beneath our feet. To be in a partnership with life again.

Simple practices can return us when we are stuck. Coming back to your senses by noticing something new in your surroundings, a slow breath in and out, or wiggling your toes. Naming one thing you're grateful for. These are not trivial, they are paddles we can utilize to push ourselves back into the main flow of the river. Presence isn't a task or a finish line; it's a lifestyle. It's okay to try again and again before it becomes natural, that's what having a practice is all about.

The good news is: we can change the world. One mind at a time. One moment at a time. When we come home to ourselves, we bring more honesty, kindness, and wisdom to everything we touch. And that ripple can impact others, those they interact with, and beyond.

Change is Necessary

We have arrived at a time when change is not just inevitable, it is essential. For too long, we have allowed systems shaped by profit, control, and fear to dictate how we live, what we believe, and who we become. We've been told what success should look like. What we should value. What we should chase. And in the process, many of us have become disconnected from our own inner compass.

Greed has been allowed to grow unchecked, often disguised as protection or progress. Progress is great, but when it's not monitored for undertones of greed, we see the effects: widening inequality, environmental degradation, health crises, mental exhaustion, and communities fraying under the weight of division. Systems meant to support us from healthcare, education, politics, to the overall economy are showing strain, revealing foundational cracks where care, balance, and responsibility was supposed to have been built in.

These issues are complex, but not immovable. The good news is: we can directly influence them. Not by waiting for someone else to save us, but by choosing our own actions with more awareness. Every purchase, every conversation, every boundary, every truth told contributes to a larger shift. As we act from a place of clarity and integrity, we begin to reshape not just our own lives, but the systems and leaders we choose to support.

The path forward doesn't require perfection. It requires intention. It requires asking for more of ourselves and also of those in power. And it starts simply, with a willingness to stop going along with what no longer feels right, and to start moving in the direction of something better.

Change is Limited

In all of this it is still significant to remember, you are only one person.

Sometimes, extraordinary individuals spark massive, visible change through movements, revolutions, inventions, and global awakenings. If that is your calling, you are an outlier and may these words also support your courage and vision. But most people change the world in quieter ways. Through the choices they make each day. Through the values they uphold. Through the way they raise their children, tend their communities, and speak the truth they can see in their daily lives.

Not every ripple is a tidal wave. And that doesn't make it any less important.

In a world that often celebrates grand gestures, let this chapter be your permission to make humble, meaningful, and consistent ones. The ones that may not trend online, but that shift the tone of your home. That invites someone else to feel safe, or seen, or hopeful. Even when it takes time to compound and show impacts, you continue. Even when you don't see the outcomes, you know it's right.

We also need to acknowledge: your time and energy is limited. Your focus has boundaries. It's just a part of being human. This means the more clearly you choose what changes you want to support or create, the more powerfully you can show up for them. Not everything needs your "yes." Your discernment is a tool. Your "no" is also an important part of achieving more of what matters to you personally.

Don't underestimate the impact of a small, conscious decision made again and again. That's how rivers shape land. That's how culture shifts. That's how healing spreads from one open mind, and one honest heart, to the next.

Navigating with Compassion

You don't need to dominate the water. You can learn to steer with patience and with grace. This is true of your interactions with others, and also with yourself, though sometimes that can be the most challenging. Taking more responsibility and also being more nurturing and caring with yourself is a difficult balance to maintain. Although it may be a challenge, you can do it, through an ongoing choice to meet yourself with curiosity and self-respect. You can remember why you are kind to yourself now; that it supports building who you've chosen to become. Earlier in this book, we spoke of a compass. That compass is not a rigid map, but an instrument of alignment. It helps you wonder back when you lose sight of the shoreline. This is much more manageable when it includes a practice of compassion. Steps are less heavy, when your heart is lighter.

Healing is not a single stop destination. Balancing an entire system doesn't happen with one drastic change. It sways, circles, doubles back, rests, repeats, and surges. The power is not in achieving the impossible, but creating beauty today. This builds into a habit, noticing beauty in more places than yesterday. It is in choosing, again and again, to return to your breath, to your values, and kindness.

You will drift, that is to be expected. What matters is how gently and how often you paddle back toward yourself. Our culture will be imperfect, what matters is that we choose what we are practicing and creating. Once we actively decide what we want to be putting out in the world, then we can simply do our best to contribute this way each day.

Living as Part of the Ecosystem

You are not the only one in this river. Healing is not a private journey. Your presence impacts your surroundings. It reshapes relationships, families, friendships, influences communities, and in time, it shifts culture. When we become better, we improve our environment. When we put forth effort into the larger ecosystem through our lives, habits, and values, this pays us back in personal growth and both internal and external healing.

The truth is, our world is moving very fast. It is not always in harmony with nature. We've allowed greed and unchecked consumption to pull us out of natural synchronicities and connections. We've allowed the trade of sustainability for speed, depth for performance, and collective well-being for personal gain. It's not our fault, but it is our responsibility to at least try to be a part of the solution.

With great freedom comes great responsibility. We have more power than ever to shape our world through the choices we make. It's our job to choose consciously. To ask ourselves what we want to support with our money, our time, and our attention.

We need to grow our culture into one that honors balance, where innovation walks hand-in-hand with sustainability. Where success includes rest, and where living well includes caring for each other and our surroundings.

This means valuing holistic and natural approaches to wellness. Our bodies are always trying to heal us, they've just been bombarded with unnatural foods, products, and lifestyles. It means living with morality and with virtue. It also means expecting the same from others whether they're individuals, companies, or leaders. A thriving culture is built not only on what we consume, but on what we nourish.

A change in culture doesn't begin with power struggles or harsh declarations. It begins in shifting waters. With a few of us deciding to move. To encourage one another. Rather than trying to force away what we don't like, identifying what we do care about. To create a new current that carries more than just ourselves. One that can carry us where we want to go together.

<u>Reflection</u>:

- What change do you want, and what's one step toward it?

- Where in your life do you feel disconnection from your values?

- Where do you feel the most connection?

- What are you ready to stop supporting with your energy?

- How can you choose better alignment in a tangible way today?

- What shifts do you hope for, and how are you involved?

- What do you want to see more of in the world?

Chapter Summary

Life will always offer new currents. This is true both within us, and around us. We are all responsible for who we choose to be. This influences what we can bring into the world. We are not responsible for what others choose, but the way our way of being could potentially impact them. We have less power than we need, but more power than we know.

The more we hold ourselves to live by morals and principles, the more we subtly change the world around us as an effect. The more we challenge ourselves to grow, the more strength we have to bring about that which we intend. Yet, we can't meet our full potential unless we give ourselves love along the journey. It's wonderful, but complex, to choose to accept yourself as you are while striving to become better.

One mind at a time, we can grow. As that growth compounds, together, we can turn the tides.

Chapter 12: The Stream You Choose

The Journey Behind You

Let's take a moment to look back. Notice where you were, compared to where you are now. You can choose any point in your life to reflect on. It could be when you started reading this book, a year ago, ten years ago, whatever feels relevant. Take inventory of the questions you carried and challenges you were working on. Remember the knots you slowly untangled. The courage it took to keep searching for areas to improve yourself. Feel grateful to yourself for your choice to pick up this book. When you chose to read this, you didn't just read another book, you engaged in a process. You met parts of yourself you had tucked away. You loosened beliefs that felt immovable. You reconnected with something deeper, steadier, and wiser within yourself.

Now, here you are today. You have room to relate differently to your thoughts, your habits, your emotions, and your story. This space can be used however you want. You have deepened your roots, reached further, and grown. Most importantly, you showed up for yourself and the world around you by choosing to work on yourself.

Wiser Waters

There will always be many types of currents in life. Whether they are your old beliefs, your circumstances, influences, or emotions, they will be pulling you in various directions. Some currents are gentle and affirming, while others can be distracting or turbulent. But you are not helpless in these waters.

With time and reflection, you can gain the strength to stand upright in the shallow, chaotic, places. You can learn when it's time to rest, and how to traverse into calmer waters. You can also swim deeper or into more expansive waters, gathering the fortitude and stamina to move yourself towards where you want to go next. As your focus sharpens and your intentions align, your direction becomes clearer and your effort more effective. Wisdom lies not in controlling the water, but in learning how to choose to move within it.

This means intentionally shaping your external world, who you spend time with, what you prioritize, what you focus on, as well as transforming your internal world. You can absolutely cultivate a mindset where your thoughts support you more often than they resist. Where you are no longer driven by fear or self-criticism, but grounded in alignment and self-trust. Inviting your mind to become a partner, not an adversary. When your inner current flows in alignment with your values, everything moves with more ease.

You may not always find yourself in perfect conditions. But with wisdom, you can keep steering toward waters that support your energy, your growth, and your peace. You can also become exceedingly more in command of your internal currents, those impacting you through your beliefs, self-talk, and focus. This results in more control of the actions you take in the world.

Returning to Life

Healing isn't equivalent to completing a checklist. It's not about fixing yourself until nothing hurts or falters. It's about reclaiming all of you, even the parts you once rejected. To be whole means to hold space for both your sadness and your joy. Your ability to acknowledge both for what they are. You can investigate the truths of your past and allow yourself to feel what comes up, while still holding the intention to move towards resolution. Your doubts can coexist with clarity, as it washes in. Your imperfections don't cancel out your progress.

You will still drift sometimes and have off days. But when you remember your compass, you are never truly lost. This journey isn't about transcending life. It is about returning to it with a new perspective, new strength, and an open heart. One able to welcome openness because you better know how to protect and heal it when you face difficulties. You are invited to live. Not as someone with everything figured out, but as someone willing to stay awake.

You are not here only to perform your healing or to become "good enough". You are here to inhabit your life. You can love yourself today, and still push yourself for a better tomorrow. You can sing and dance, cry and laugh, struggle and overcome, and it's all a part of your own unique and beautiful journey.

Building Your Life

You are not in a race, you are in a river.

Let your growth come in cycles. Let your energy rise and recede like tides. Let your life include space to pause, breathe, and start again. We live in a world that confuses urgency with importance. But the most meaningful transformations happen slowly, through meaningful engagement and consistency. You can choose to take steps towards a way of being that nourishes you. One that lets you sustain joy, not just survive stress.

What would happen if you stopped believing you are who you were, and started believing you are who you choose to be now?

Who you were was shaped by many things: your upbringing, your surroundings, your circumstances, and the beliefs you were handed before you ever knew you could question them. But today, you are aware. That means you have the power to participate in shaping who you become. This version of you is better equipped to build a life that brings you fulfillment.

Transformation begins not with what others see, but with what you decide to believe. If you keep returning to your old story, reiterating your old identity, you'll keep walking in circles. But the moment you say, "I get to choose", a new door opens. That belief is not denial of your past, it's a reclaiming of your present moment. As a result, also the reclaiming of your future.

You might not always feel like the strongest version of yourself or most in tune with your vision. Changing a belief is not about pretending. It's about choosing to invest in the belief that your growth is already possible, and letting that intention lead you to finding the right path. You don't have to fake confidence. You just have to walk in the direction of your values, even when you're uncertain how you will get there. If you can't fully believe you are the version of yourself that you want yet, then focus on believing you can become that person. What we speak to ourselves becomes easier to believe and feel over time. So if the words still feel empty, give yourself grace. Let them be a practice, not proof, and trust that resonance will build as you return to them with sincerity. They will become more natural in time. Just try again, thank yourself for staying on the path, and choose to trust the process.

When you believe you are becoming who you choose, your focus shifts. You notice different perspectives, options, and capabilities within yourself. What seemed impossible starts to make you curious, and then look interesting, and then eventually look reachable. Opportunities you were shut off to, or that you didn't even know existed, start to take space in your awareness. Then with enough practice, they start to become new possibilities and habits.

Staying Connected to the Compass

Your compass doesn't require batteries or some kind of magic. It only requires your attention. I'm not trying to make any of this sound easy, because it's not. I'm trying to remind you that it's truly possible with a practice. But a practice does not mean short-lived trials of new things, it means long-term dedication. This doesn't mean rigid thinking. You can commit while still being receptive and what resonates over time. If the same practice does, stick with it, even when results are still far down the path. If adjustments feel right for you, reshape it to be something you can stick to. But do stick to something you believe in.

You get to choose what you keep. You don't need external evidence or permission. When you consistently invest in what you value, the meaning and momentum grow from within. You can make space for any practices that reconnect you to your sense of inner truth. Here are just a few examples:

- Quiet mornings or walks
- Journaling
- Honest conversations
- Time in nature
- Calming music

- Listening for resonance within yourself

- Asking meaningful questions and making space to listen

- Breathing deeply and calmly

It can feel a bit radical to live by your own values in a world that sometimes profits from your doubt. It takes courage to be open and gain the necessary strength to get through it all, instead of shutting down. To learn and know when to push yourself, but also when to rest even if others rush. To practice curiosity when it would be easier to defend or avoid change. Your bravery won't always be loud or perceived as such by others. It's still worthwhile.

Sometimes it looks like saying *no* when you're expected to say *yes*. Like speaking gently in a world that rewards dominance. Like showing up with honesty, even when you're afraid it won't be received well. It can look like not abandoning yourself, even when others around you are struggling to connect, be honest, and aligned. Where their expectation is for you to follow suit, and not ask the kinds of questions that make them uncomfortable. It can be hard for people on the path to explain to others who resist change. But your path doesn't need to match theirs. You can find your own balance of growth and peace. You have the freedom to choose where you flow.

Accessing the Flow

Flow doesn't mean ease without effort. It means openness and maintaining connection to your truth. It is not a lucky accident or a fleeting burst of momentum, it's something that can be cultivated through consistency, honesty, and maintaining your intentions.

Flow is earned through the quiet, sometimes messy work of making decisions aligned with your values. It's the result of trimming distractions, meeting your needs, and building systems around you that reflect the life you actually want. It happens when your intuitive mind, your attention, and your goals all begin to move in harmony. While it doesn't erase the requirement of putting in effort, it does transform it. Flow grows through continued practice. When you take action from a place of authenticity, your energy carries farther, and the effort you make becomes more effective. It is then more sustainable and more powerful.

You don't have to force change. When you choose truth and follow it with aligned action, change begins to unfold. The stream you choose matters. Choose one that feels honest. One that brings you more fully into embracing life, even when it challenges you. When you move with integrity and presence, the current you flow within begins to recognize you, and it rises to meet you on your adventure.

Chapter Summary

You are the one steering your life. While there will still be rapids and rocks, you have deepened something within yourself that can help you no matter where you go. Trust in your own capacity and recognition of your choice gives you power in directing where you take yourself next.

Reflection:

- What belief have I released that once felt immovable?

- What parts of me have I reclaimed?

- What does staying connected to my compass look like?

- Who do I choose to be in this life?

- What life do I choose to create?

You don't have to be fearless to move forward. You just have to remember that you get to decide where you go. From there, and each day, simply keep going.

A Final Offering

Before this book fully closes, I want to share something personal with you. Not long ago, I had a vivid dream that stayed with me. In it, I caught a strange and silent white fish, unlike anything I'd seen before. It carried a kind of weightless wisdom, a quiet presence that didn't ask to be held, only noticed. When I released it, I felt changed. Not because of what I had done, but because of what I had witnessed.

The dream felt meaningful in a way I couldn't fully explain, but I tried in a poem soon after. I've come to see it as a symbol of grace; of the truths that don't need to be solved or claimed, only honored.

So as a final thank you for walking through these pages with me, I offer it here to you. May it meet you in your own waters, wherever you are in the current.

The White Fish

I cast my line in quiet thought,
Where winding streams and daydreams caught.
The flicker-fins of common things,
Bright silver shapes with tugging wings.

But then, a pull both sharp and still,
A silent weight against my will.
I drew it forth, and in the sun,
Beheld a fish like none I'd won.

Its body gleamed in ancient white,
Like marble carved from shadowed light.
It did not thrash. It did not plead.
It bore no hunger, lacked all need.

Its eyes were closed. Its mouth was sealed.
Yet something vast it half-revealed.
A presence born of other streams,
A wisdom deeper than my dreams.

I saw within its lion shape,
No beast, no prey, no call to take.
But something fierce and stone-engraved,
That asked not to be healed, but saved.

The moment swelled. I could not speak.
My heart grew soft. My hands grew weak.
I felt the reverence, sharp and dear.
What was not mine to hold was clear.

No glory waits for catching grace,
I gave it back to water's space.
It did not turn. It did not flee.
It simply was, and flowed past me.

And though I stood there on the shore,
I sensed I wasn't me before.
Not seeking more, not craving proof,
But still beneath a deeper truth.

Thank You

I hope this book helps lead you towards more discernment, self-directed responsibility, and freedom in your life.

You can share these ideas with others by leaving a review:

With gratitude,

Forest of Truth

If you would like a daily reminded of this message, check out these *Out of the Current* inspired 100% organic cotton t-shirts:

GROW THYSELF

Interested in more support for your journey?

Consider self-improvement coaching: